From The Editors of **COM**

The Beginner's Guide To Buying A Personal Computer

By
Richard Mansfield
Myron D. Miller
Kathleen E. Martinek
and
Robert Lock

Published by **COMPUTE! Books**,
A Division of Small System Services, Inc.,
Greensboro, North Carolina

Printed in the United States of America

ISBN 0-942386-22-1

10 9 8 7 6 5 4 3 2

COMPUTE! Books is a division of Small System Services, Inc., Publishers of **COMPUTE!** Magazine
Editorial Offices are located at:
505 Edwardia Drive, Greensboro, NC 27409 USA. (919) 275-9809

Introduction . . . . Page iv

Part One: **How To Buy Your First Computer** . . . . Page 1
   Terminology And Fundamentals: An Overview . . . . Page 5
   The Computer . . . . Page 5
   Displays . . . . Page 6
   Storage Devices . . . . Page 6
   Programs And Programming . . . . Page 7
   The Learning Process . . . . Page 9
   Other Resources . . . . Page 10

Part Two: **Should You Buy A Computer?** . . . . Page 15
   Wants Versus Needs . . . . Page 17
   Will You Enjoy Programming? . . . . Page 18
   Justifying A Purchase . . . . Page 22
   Buying For Your Business . . . . Page 23
   Warranties . . . . Page 24

Part Three: **Shopping For A Computer** . . . . Page 27
   Memory . . . . Page 29
   Some Memory Must Change . . . . Page 31
   Screen Format . . . . Page 36
   Keyboards . . . . Page 41
   Graphics And Character Sets . . . . Page 45
   Languages . . . . Page 48
   Color . . . . Page 50
   Software . . . . Page 51
   Documentation . . . . Page 52
   Peripherals . . . . Page 52
   Bringing It Home . . . . Page 55

Personal Computer Specification Charts And Analysis . . . Page 60
Manufacturers . . . . Page 80
Larger System Vendors . . . . Page 81
Glossary . . . . Page 82

Introduction

Robert Lock
Editor/Publisher, **COMPUTE!** Publications

This book grew out of a group effort initiated by a series of articles proposed by Myron D. Miller for **COMPUTE!** Magazine. With his initial articles in hand, and the combined writing and editing of Richard Mansfield, Assistant Editor of **COMPUTE!**, Kathleen Martinek, Managing Editor, Charles Brannon, Editorial Assistant, and myself, we've endeavored to produce a Beginner's Guide that will strip away some of the mystery of personal computers. The first two sections of the book try to give you a brief overview of the personal computers, and help you analyze your interests. Part Three of the book is intended to teach you the basics of computer components and terminology. You should expect to be able to thoroughly evaluate personal computers upon completion and understanding of the third section.

Section Three concludes with a set of charts matching the topic areas covered in that section. These charts, while not intended to "rate" or "rank" computers, will allow you to easily compare and evaluate the features most important to you in a personal computer.

Special thanks to the Production Staff at **COMPUTE!** Publications, and to Harry Blair, our talented illustrator.

How To Buy Your First Computer

Part One

Do you need to know which computer is the best one for your family or your office? Do you want to know which computer plays the best video games or which can maintain your business inventory? Are you interested in computing, but find the going rough? You face a mountain of information.

This booklet is for the beginner who has not yet bought a computer. It is designed to help you make an intelligent buying decision and a good investment.

We'll cover the following important topics: learning about computers, deciding if you need a computer, and how to make your most effective purchase. At the end of the book, you'll find specifications for many of the most popular personal computers, computers with prices ranging from $98.00 to over $3000.00. By the time you reach the third part of this book, you'll be able to understand some of the reasons for those price distinctions, and be better able to evaluate your own needs. This book is not a consumer's guide to specific brands. It is a guide to helping you look at your own expectations about personal computing, and then match those expectations to products that are currently available.

The ability of our technology to place cost effective personal computers in our schools, offices, and homes is a recent development. The personal computer market has grown up in a relatively short time, with the first entrants appearing only five years ago. In that time, we've seen an increasing awareness of what's been called the *consumer* computer. If your vision of a personal computer includes midnight sessions with manuals and a soldering iron, you're out of touch. The personal computers of today are increasingly like appliances, with user friendly features and attention to the needs of the "human-machine interaction."

Microcomputers have brought a mysterious, generous technology into the homes of everyday people. Only a few years ago, computers were huge, extremely expensive, and complex. They were kept locked in special cool, dustfree rooms. The rooms were filled with gleaming plastic and whirring disks; the machines were tended by an exclusive elite. It was a science fiction priesthood, a religion from the future. Only the largest institutions and industries could afford to buy and operate them. Until recently the public has had little contact with computing and, as a result, still knows relatively little about computers.

Buying a computer is something like buying a television station or a supersonic jet — assuming that these items suddenly became affordable. You are about to buy a very sophisticated (though remarkably sturdy) machine. It is still essentially mysterious. That is, we do not easily understand computers on the same level that we understand automobiles or washing machines. We do have highly sophisticated items in our homes already (microwave ovens, televisions), but the main difference between the TV and the computer is the level of knowledge required to intelligently purchase and use them.

Does it sound as if you have your work cut out for you? Here's just a bit of additional bad news. There's that mountain of information we mentioned earlier. Perhaps it would be more accurate to call it a volcano, erupting new information continuously. The personal computing industry has exploded and new products, programs, techniques, and ideas flow out at an amazing rate. The dynamics of the industry make the computer field confusing, but exciting. One thing is certain, you will need to learn a few things before making your final selection.

Four Major Areas   In the remaining portion of Part I, we'll cover the following topics:

Terminology and fundamentals
Applications and operation
Programming a computer
Resources and assistance

Terminology and Fundamentals Your personal computer has three basic operating components. The interaction of these three components, and an understanding of their design and abilities, will go a long way toward helping you get an overview for decision making. The three major components are the computer, the computer display, and the storage facility. Within each of these primary categories are dozens of secondary ones. Let's start with a discussion of generic capabilities.

The Computer ROM. (Read Only Memory: permanent memory that's "programmed" by the manufacturer and is not alterable by the user.) ROM contains your computer's basic "personality"; when you type something on your computer keyboard, and it appears on the screen, you don't have to "tell" your computer to write to the screen. The computer's operating system programs, embedded in ROM, automatically handle this for you.

RAM. (Random Access Memory: memory that's available in your computer for "working" storage.) This is memory that you use each time you work with your computer. When you type a program, or set of instructions, into your computer, this is where your computer saves them. You don't have to worry about how it saves them (your ROM based programs take care of this). What you do need to remember is that, unlike ROM, RAM is not permanent memory. Thus, when you turn your computer off, RAM is erased. That's the reason your computer has external storage devices available. We'll get to these in a few paragraphs, but first let's cover displays.

Displays Your display is your window into your computer. If you had no TV screen or monitor, using your computer would be like typing on a typewriter with no paper. The type of display you have is equally important. If your computer has color graphics capabilities, then you'll need to be considering a color television or monitor for it. Otherwise a less expensive black and white TV will do. We strongly recommend that you take a look at various displays with your computer. Buying an expensive personal computer system, and then hooking it up to the cheapest TV you can find may be somewhat like buying $19.00 speakers for your $2000.00 stereo. After all, it is the display that you'll spend all of your working time looking at.

Some computers come with a built-in display monitor. This standard feature should be another consideration in your decision.

Storage Devices In our discussion of RAM, we concluded with the need to have something available for storing the contents of RAM when you turn the computer off. This isn't, of course, the only reason for storage. This is where you'll end up saving the hundreds of programs you'll acquire and develop for your computer. There are two major types of storage available. One is cassette tape, the other diskettes. The cassette tape type of storage is a medium we're all familiar with. You simply plug a tape into your recorder and tell your computer to save or load something. Operation of a disk drive is equally simple. The major difference between these two technologies is cost. Your simple disk storage system will add at least $300-$400 to the cost of your system; your tape based storage will add less than $100. You'll have to weigh this cost disparity against your needs. Tape is much, much slower than disk, in its loading and saving operations. In some personal computer systems it is less reliable. Disks have the advantage of much greater storage capacity, a factor essential to some educational applications, and such business ones as data management, word processing, and so on. Again, as with the computer display you select, you'll be living with the storage medium you select. Evaluate carefully! Your initial choice isn't a one way street, of course. Many home users start off with tape storage, and "move-up" in several months to disk storage. This is an ideal way to spread out the costs of your initial personal computer system.

Other Factors We've briefly covered the major components of your new system. You should have a general idea now of what's involved in defining your system. There are other important considerations as well. We'll delve more deeply into these topics in Part III of this book, and cover topics such as amount of RAM (i.e., the size of your computer's memory), the keyboard (touch-style versus flat), peripherals (printers, modems, speech synthesizers, graphics output devices), and more detailed coverage of the above areas. For now, you have your overview. Let's look at the more theoretical side of computers.

Programs and Programming Programming means using a programming language (BASIC, FORTRAN, COBOL, PASCAL, PILOT, etc.) to instruct the computer, to tell it what you want it to do. You cannot (alas) simply type: "Please make me a list of the even numbers between 1 and 100." Instead, you type: "FOR I = 2 TO 100 STEP 2: PRINT I: NEXT I." This is an example of BASIC (Beginner's All-Purpose Symbolic Instruction Code), and it's one of the languages used most frequently in talking to personal computers.

Do you have to know how to program a computer in order to use it? No. But you will be dependent on others to provide you with software (programs). You can buy programs already on tape or disk, and you can find many in magazines that you'll need to type into your computer and save on tape or disk. Programming is very useful, but is programming for you? Purchased software may not meet your specific requirements, or you may have an application in mind for which no software exists. What do you do then? Some people find programming tedious and boring. Many find it challenging and fascinating. If you're expecting to use your computer system in your small business, you may not have the time to develop your own programs. After all, you're expecting the computer to save you time, right? Be prepared to buy commercially available software, regardless of whether you've decided you want to learn programming.

Programs (and general software capabilities) are a critical part of your new computer system. Indeed, one is useless without the other. Limitations in either hardware or software are limitations to the whole. Knowing something about programming is very useful in choosing a machine. Quite often, the various computers differ in their language features. Personal computers are not (unfortunately) like the record industry. You can't pick up the latest "hit program" and automatically expect it to work on your computer. As you've probably learned to expect by now, there are exceptions to this, and Part III will help you understand the differences.

If all of these caveats sound discouraging, cheer-up. We're just touching all the bases, trying to give you an

idea of the mass of information in front of you. The world of personal computing is truly turning into one of consumer computing. As an aware, informed consumer, you'll make a wiser choice.

The Learning Process We have looked into some of the areas you need to learn about. How do you learn all this? Our first suggestion will be learn first, buy later. Don't be in a hurry to part with your cash. Try to get a feel for what you'll be using a computer for. Doubtless, many additional uses will come to you when you own a computer, but try to imagine it working in your den or office. Are you really that interested in computers? If you're not sure, don't buy until you are. If and when you do decide to buy, then begin a detailed comparison of the various machines. Last, buy the best machine you can afford that meets your needs. Simply put, know what you are buying.

Other Resources Obviously, we expect this book to get you started in your learning process. By the time you finish, you'll be able to ask informed questions, make intelligent comparisons, and begin to examine your own needs. There are many other sources of information and help as well. Here are our suggestions. As with anything else in computing, try a logical approach. Establish a hierarchy for learning. Start with simple concepts and definitions and work your way up.

Do not get involved with "graduate studies" in any one area; that is, don't go too deep. You don't have to know transistor theory, FORTRAN, or machine architecture to be able to make an intelligent decision about computers.

Discuss what you have learned with other people interested in computing. If you can question an experienced computer buff, you can learn much. Discussion with other beginners is also valuable.

Where do you learn about computing? Fortunately, there are a number of sources of information.

Books And Magazines Books and magazines are an excellent source of information. However, each medium has its problems. Books are usually somewhat dated. Remember our heaving volcano, erupting under the pressure of a technological explosion. While a book is being published, the industry keeps progressing. Hence, when the book is released for sale it may already be somewhat behind the times. This fact is not critical when you are studying the fundamentals, but bear in mind that any book published six or seven years ago will probably be quite dated. Check the copyright date on all books.

However, books can teach you programming before you have a computer. There are many fine books on BASIC and the other languages used in computing. A book will introduce the rules of the language and programming concepts, and you can write your own programs from the principles covered in the book.

This is not an ideal learning situation. However, bear in mind the objective: to get a sufficient introduction to programming to allow you to make a decision. Do you want to pursue the programming aspect of computing or not?

Magazines, on the other hand, are usually up to date, but it is often hit or miss whether a magazine will have any articles that are useful to beginners. Obviously, a magazine cannot repeat articles over and over in order to catch all of the newcomers.

Clubs And Users Groups This is probably one of the best places to learn. You can ask questions. You will meet people who range in experience from machine language wizards to other beginners. You will get a variety of perspectives on computing, applications, and the choice of machines. Also, you may be able to get some hands-on experience with a machine. Contact with other people will round out your learning, fill in the holes, and correct misconceptions. The advice that you can get is invaluable. You should not be ashamed of the fact that you are a beginner. The best thing to do is to admit that you are a beginner, and start picking the wizards' brains. People, by nature, like to impart their wisdom. Most people will answer questions for you. So, ask away.

Schools You can attend formal courses at colleges and technical schools, if you have the time and money. However, this type of training is more for career opportunities. Much of what is taught is not applicable to personal computing anyway. Look for informal adult continuing education classes offered by colleges and high schools. Tuition is usually reasonable and, while non-credit, such classes could be a very good source of information. Also keep an eye out for lectures or symposiums.

Dealers Dealers are a good source of information. They can demonstrate the machines, answer questions, and give advice on peripherals and software. But, remember, the dealer wants to sell you a computer, not give you an education. To be fair, if you expect the dealer to spend his time with you, is it not reasonable for the dealer to expect an eventual purchase from you?

Manufacturers The individual computer manufacturers can provide you with information concerning their particular machine. This is a good source for material to make product comparisons. Sales brochures will highlight the major features of the machine. Of course, bear in mind that a manufacturer is not going to tell you that the keyboard is awkward to use or that the screen vibrates. Negative information such as this can be found in magazine reviews or from experienced users. When writing to manufacturers, mention in your letter that you desire information on the specifications and features of their machine.

Shows And Exhibitions If you live close to a major city, watch for computer shows, exhibitions, or fairs. The manufacturers, software companies, and dealers set up booths and display their products. Some shows offer seminars and speeches, sometimes conducted by computing legends. At a computer show, you can watch demonstrations, get your hands on a keyboard, pick up a great amount of literature, and maybe find some good buys on equipment. You will probably leave the show dazzled and somewhat smarter than when you came.

The above sources of information are some trails to follow in your climb up the mountain of information. Which one should you use? If possible, use all of them. The more perspectives you can get on computing, the better prepared you will be for making a decision on a machine.

Don't waste time with material that is over your head, and don't go into things too deeply. You need a broad, but shallow, coverage of the subject to get started.

You can delve into specific areas later. Avoid frustration. You will have to accept the fact that there are going to be things that you do not understand right away. Be patient and keep learning; it will come.

Should You Buy A Computer?

Let's try to simplify the most basic question: should you buy a computer?

There are several issues to consider, so here are a few questions to mull over. They are meant as guidelines to aid in predicting the likelihood that you would use and enjoy a computer in your home.

Do you *need* a computer? If you do, for what purpose? How would the computer solve a problem for you (in business? in education?).

What would be the advantage of using the computer rather than a conventional method of doing the same thing?

Will using a computer justify the cost of the machine and any necessary accessory devices such as a printer?

Do you *want* a computer? Why? Are you interested in computing itself, in programming? Do you have a child who would benefit from early familiarity with computers? Do you enjoy playing arcade games?

Wants Versus Needs The idea here is to focus on underlying motivations. What motives are leading you toward a possible purchase? Are you forced to get a computer because your business will no longer be competitive if you don't? Are you thinking of saving some money by owning some arcade games instead of dropping quarters into Space Invaders at the shopping center game room? Did you spend months rediscovering the pleasures of math after you bought your first calculator?

If you can isolate the reasons you are interested in computing, you can more clearly establish whether or not you should buy a computer at this time. The questions divide into two entirely separate zones: *want* versus *need*. Either of them is a good reason to purchase, but they are different reasons.

Let's briefly evaluate your answers. If you answered "no," there is no clear *need,* you are predicting that the computer would serve you in no obviously practical, necessary way at the present time. It might also mean that you simply have not yet realized the ways in which a computer would assist you at work or, in some cases, *become* your new job. One woman wrote into **COMPUTE!** describing a "transformation" in her life. She had been an accountant, working for a large firm in the Midwest. Last year she bought a home computer and discovered that she could get as much work done at home as she did using the office's larger computer. What's more, she could save babysitting, transportation, and other expenses.

After several months, during which she took on some clients of her own after work, she quit her job and is now working for herself full-time. Alvin Toffler, in his book *The Third Wave,* describes new "cottage" industries rising up in the coming decades. Many of the reasons that people now commute to work are becoming obsolete as computers and advanced types of telephones and televisions make it increasingly easier for people to work at home.

If you can clearly justify the purchase of a computer on such grounds, you need only try to gain enough understanding of computer specifications and terminology to make a cost-effective purchase. If you can say you need a computer, you are ready to go on to Part III where we look into the considerations involved in making a final choice between models.

Those who could not say that they "need a computer," should not feel that their "desire" for a computer is in any sense inferior to someone else's demonstrable "need." If you sense that a computer would improve your life or fascinate you (or your child) — this is perhaps one of the very best justifications to buy one. People who merely need computing might not like needing it. They might wish they didn't have to associate with it. If you are enthusiastic, though, you will give the computer your attention and it will richly reward you.

A refrigerator goes about its business regardless of whether you are around or not. But a computer is a "problem-solving" machine. It computes. It plays games, but it also manages information. In order to do these things, it requires attention, it requires a problem to solve (from you), and it will flourish if you can program.

Will You Enjoy Programming? An important factor is your interest in computing itself and how likely you are to enjoy programming. Programming is problem solving using a precise language. There are, though, many misconceptions about what programming involves. Do you need to know advanced mathematics? No. Many of the best programmers have only the usual high school background: a little algebra and geometry. And you don't even need that. Children learn to program.

It's interesting that a large computer firm, when

looking for programmers, found that music majors and English majors were frequently the best programmers. Solving a problem on a computer seems to involve two types of thinking: creativity and precision. And the emphasis is on creativity.

Another misconception is that you can damage the computer by making an error in programming. If you make an error, the computer will notify you on the screen that you goofed, but nothing will happen to the machine. It is the same with the pocket calculator: if you try to multiply one billion by one billion, you will exceed the calculator's limits. It can't count that high; it will probably say "error" or display a symbol for "overflow." But it won't explode.

BASIC is the standard language which comes with nearly every home computer. One of the best things about programming in BASIC is that it has many "error messages." If your program fails to work right the first time (and nearly everyone's does) your computer

will *show you where and why* there is a problem. BASIC is friendly to the programmer.

Home computers have their limits too. If you tried to multiply 100 billion times 100 billion, the computer would print something like this:

OVERFLOW ERROR IN LINE 30

and you would then know where and why your program stopped working.

People of all ages and all backgrounds have become good programmers. You interact with the computer and, when you make a mistake, no damage is done. You just type over your error and that's it.

Larger, more complex programs, though, can require hours or days of concentrated work. Although the computer will be there to point out many of your errors, it cannot make the corrections. It is misleading to think that you will be writing a program to manage your business inventory within hours of bringing home your computer. You could learn to operate an inventory program within hours if you *bought* a pre-written program, but you can't create the program yourself that quickly.

Most people find that it takes several weeks to become reasonably familiar with BASIC. True speed and skill can require several months of part-time programming practice and study. So, if you are in doubt that you have the available time or could sustain the interest, you might want to think a bit more about whether you will enjoy programming. Or at least be prepared to buy most of your software.

But if you like learning new things, chances are excellent that you will find a computer the best investment you ever made. These machines are the most patient, most personal of teachers. It sounds strange to call a computer a *personal* teacher. Most people imagine that computers are cold, unforgiving, even, somehow, hostile. Hundreds of movies have contributed to the image of the computer as monster, running amok at the slightest provocations.

This image is not accurate. True, computers do *seem* to cause problems — we frequently hear it on the news: "computer error sends Toledo man $20,000 electric bill." The fact is that a human made this error. Computers are not mind readers — somebody forgot to type in the decimal point when they entered $200.00 into the computer at the electric company. A computer

is a tool, like a frying pan, and it cannot be blamed for being fed incorrect information. If your eggs were too salty, would you blame the pan or the cook? Nevertheless, the image persists.

In truth, computers make magnificent teachers: they have infinite patience and they let you know at once if you're right or wrong. They are available at any hour and for as long as you care to work with them. They will respond at your level of understanding and they allow you to go at your own pace. So, if you enjoy discovering new things, adding new skills, learning to compute at home can be the most pleasant educational experience you'll ever have.

The questions in this chapter are, of course, rather arbitrary and are only designed to make you consider potential areas of concern. With many of the personal computers on the market today — the presence of children in the home, aged two or three and up, is ample justification for buying a home computer. The computer is capable of providing much more flexible learning and gaming activities than those provided by television.

Justifying A Purchase Some purchases are justified fairly easily: food, shelter, transportation. They are practical necessities in the modern world. Except for business applications, a home computer is rarely *necessary* at this point. It might even seem to be a luxury. But the computers are coming and you will ignore them at your peril.

The interesting thing about our list of necessities above is that "transportation" would not have been on that list a century ago. Modern life has adjusted to easy transportation, things have spread out. The clothing store is south of town, school is north, that

good restaurant is ten miles from home. When the
internal combustion engine was developed, the layout
of life changed. New, hard roads were built
everywhere.

Today, to service the needs of computers, aerials
go up, cables are installed, satellites rocket into orbit.
Schools are buying them by the thousands, practically
every business has them (or needs them), modern
government and defense would collapse without them.

Does your home need one? If you have children,
the answer is probably yes. They will be growing up in
a computerized society. Ignorance or fear of computing
will become a handicap in the future.

Do you need one for yourself? If the only use you
can think of is to straighten out your personal budget,
the answer would be no (or else you have a terribly
complex home financial situation.)

But if, like most people, you can think of several
uses for a home computer, you might want to start
thinking seriously about buying one. The prices might
surprise you — many cost about the same as a color TV.
One sells for less than $100.

In Part III, we will get into the practical questions
involved in selecting the right machine. We will explore
the advantages and disadvantages of the least
expensive home computers. We will also look at
features available on more luxurious models. Chances
are, if you've decided to buy, Part III will help you find
a computer which will do what you want it to. Equally
important, you can find one that won't cost so much
that you *will* need it to straighten out a financial
situation, grown suddenly complex. But, first, a few
comments about bringing computers into the business
world.

If You're Buying For Your Business Once you've
defined your own needs and expectations, do you head
for the nearest computer store and plunk down the
cash? We would suggest not. Now's the time to exercise
that same judgement you've used to get your successful

business rolling in the first place.

For you, considerations of service and support are perhaps even more critical than they are for a home or educational buyer. You're buying this machine because you expect it to take a substantial load off of key personnel. If all goes well, you'll be maximizing your staff and your own potential by bringing in an efficient, effective computer system.

You can expect to meet resistance from some of your staff who might suffer from what's politely been called "computer phobia." The more you can do to avoid these problems, the smoother your transition, and the sooner you'll be deriving those long-awaited benefits. Your decisions here, and proper respect for, and management of, your personnel during this process are as important as the computer system you end up with.

Involve key personnel in the selection process. Take them along on your computer store visits, solicit their input on software packages. If your local store(s) offer training, sit in on a class. Is it useful? Does your typist like the feel of the keyboard? Can your store provide you with references: other business men and women in similar circumstances who've successfully made the transition to a small computer? Are they happy with the training and support provided by the store?

Beyond the problems of selection and start-up, where will you and your computer system be two years from now? Have you selected a system that can grow with you? If you can cost justify the system in two years' time, then you may not need to worry about it. If you can't, then you should.

Warranties One of the considerations you might not expect to encounter is the issue of software warranties. Let's assume you pay $500.00 for a business software package called Package XYZ. For that $500.00, you get a diskette with the software on it and an extensive users' manual and documentation.

At this point, in addition to the documentation, you have a very expensive diskette. Can you "back-up" this diskette? In other words, can you load it into your computer and make a duplicate copy of it for safety?

Interestingly enough, because of problems with the theft of computer software, you may find that you can't copy this particular diskette. If something happens that accidentally destroys or damages that $4.00 or $5.00 piece of plastic (your diskette with $500.00 worth of software), what do you do if you have no back-up? You can certainly see the potential problem.

We would suggest that you carefully review software with problems such as this in mind. Again, as we've said several times in these pages, you've got to make a balanced judgement. If you can't live without Package XYZ, then obviously you have to live with the company's back-up policy, or lack of it. Generally, however, your problem won't be that cut and dried.

Almost all software vendors have a replacement policy covering damaged master diskettes. Even if you're not able to make an on-site back-up, you may, for example, be allowed to return the diskette for replacement at a modest cost ($10.00 or more, generally). If this is the case, then you have to realize that for whatever time period it takes to get your replacement, your computer system would be unable to perform those tasks for you.

Maybe that's a significant problem, maybe not. The important point is that the ability to back up software, its warranty, and recoverability, are areas of potential impact on your daily use of the computer. So evaluate them in terms of your needs and expectations.

Shopping For A Computer

We will assume you've made your decision at this point. Regardless of whether you decided you wanted a computer or need a computer, the goal of this chapter is to help you figure out what's what in computers. You won't find a recommendation for computer x over computer y. What you will find is the information necessary to help you combine our resource and "self-teaching" suggestions from Part I with some hard facts about computers in general, and most of the "consumer computers" currently (or soon to be) in the marketplace.

Remember that volcano of information we've alluded to? Well, here it comes. We're going to take you through a land of bits and bytes, pixels and hi-res graphics, computer generated "voices," CRTs and LEDs.

PIXEL? BYTE?

Sound intimidating? It really isn't. By the time we're through with this chapter, you'll know what these terms mean, and more importantly, you'll be able to decide which ones you even need to be concerned with.

Let's look at some of the considerations for choosing a machine. Some of the things we will look at

will be highly subjective. How much memory do you
need? (Remember RAM and ROM?) What display *size*
do you want? (80 columns across your screen by 25
lines?) Do you need color capabilities?

Memory How much memory do you need? There are
two basic rules regarding memory: 1. larger memories
can make complex programming more efficient, and
allow you to do more sophisticated things with your
computer. 2. larger memories are generally more
expensive. It's the familiar story: capability costs
money.

First, let's take a quick look at memory and try to
find out what memory is. Memory is a warehouse for
the storage of instructions and data within the
computer. The warehouse is divided into electronic
bins or slots called "locations" or "addresses." Each
location has a numerical identifier, unique to that
location, called its *address;* a marvelous and
surprisingly simple term in light of the industry's love
for jargon.

The processor uses the address to access (call up
or find) any particular location. Each location can
store one byte (1 byte = 8 bits, *binary* dig*its*) of
information.

What can you find in one byte? A single
alphanumeric or graphic character, part of a number,
part of an address for another memory location, or a
single instruction for the processor. As you can see, a
byte is a very small parcel of information. Thus, we
will need many memory locations. Due to the
electronics involved, microcomputers are generally
limited to 65,536 locations, thus we can potentially
store 65,536 bytes of data in the memory. Although
some microcomputers can access more memory, we'll
treat 65,536 as our "ceiling" for the following
discussion. However, not all of this memory is available
for our use. The processor requires a chunk of it for an
instruction manual.

In order to be programmable and yet also

automatically perform housekeeping chores (scanning the keyboard, loading or saving programs, displaying information on the screen, and other internal functions), the computer must have two types of memory, ROM and RAM. Both types reside in the 65,536 locations mentioned above. ROM, *Read Only Memory*, is for permanent storage. RAM, *Random Access Memory*, is temporary storage. Both ROM and RAM are random access memories. (*Random Access* – refers to the ability to access any specific location within the memory directly.) The contents of a ROM are written by the manufacturer and can never change. The computer can read the contents of a ROM, but cannot change these contents. ROMs are like a slab of granite with the information chiseled deep into the surface. RAMs are like a chalk board, the contents can be written, then read, then rewritten. This entire operation may occur in a few millionths of a second.

What is all this used for? ROMs are used for storing the operating system and the BASIC interpreter (or possibly interpreters for other "high level" languages). The microprocessor controls every function in the computer. Nothing happens unless the processor orders it. While being remarkably capable, the processor hasn't much memory. It does not remember how to do anything so we must provide an instruction manual for it. This manual is the operating system, which contains machine language programs telling the processor what to do. Also, the microprocessor does not understand any high level language such as BASIC. We must provide an *interpreter* to convert a BASIC instruction into the address of a series of *machine language* instructions, which are meaningful to the processor and which represent the BASIC instruction. Obviously, we don't want these instructions to change or disappear. They are cut into ROM memory.

Some Memory Must Change In order to program the computer, we must have a memory that *can* change: RAM. RAMs (chips) are used for the storage of our programs and variables. The processor also uses a small portion of RAM (the *stack*) for the temporary storage of addresses it needs. Another portion of RAM is usually reserved for the video display. Regardless of its use, RAM can always be changed.

You may run into the term *volatile*. This refers to RAM's nasty habit of losing the contents of the memory if power is interrupted. RAMs are volatile. ROMs are nonvolatile (if we were to lose the operating system, the computer would be useless). But, since RAMs are volatile if power is lost, even momentarily, your program vanishes. So it is wise to regularly save your program into mass storage (cassette or disk) when programming.

The usual unit of measure for memory is K bytes or simply K. 1K = 1024 locations, but just remember a 1000. Let's inspect our potential 64K (65536/1024 = 64) of memory. Allow 12 to 18K for the operating system and the BASIC interpreter. Throw in another 2 to 4K for video addresses, I/O, etc. What you have left can be used for your RAM, although the operating system will probably want some of your RAM reserved for it. You may also want to leave a little room for expansion ROM. You can put in as little RAM as you want, but you have a definite limit on the maximum amount. So our original 64K of potential memory gets whittled down to something less.

Let's take a look at what to look for in memory when you are shopping for a computer. First ROM. You may notice that the amount of ROM is sometimes advertised. Which is better, 12K of ROM or 14K? That is a fairly meaningless question. The actual amount of ROM is not, in itself, important. You can't use ROM, only the machine can.

What are important are the functions that are packed into the ROM. The ideal is a great number of powerful functions packed into the smallest total number of memory locations. So you can't shop for numbers, you have to shop for performance. ROM is something like a book, you purchase a book for its information, not how many pages it contains.

Like books, ROMs may be revised. Some manufacturers revise their operating system and BASIC. Naturally, when you buy a new machine you should expect to get the latest revision of ROM. If you are considering buying a used machine, you should investigate such revisions. Find out what limitations you will have, and how expensive upgrading would be. Usually software designed for the newer revisions is not compatible with the older revisions. Check it out first, or else the money you save on a used machine may end up being spent upgrading the ROMs.

One last thing you may want to consider. Did the manufacturer leave any space for expansion ROM? Expansion falls into two categories: 1. Assigned memory location – some portion of the 65,536 potential locations are reserved for expansion ROM. 2. Physical connection – the sockets for the expansion ROM should be wired into the circuit board (making the addition of expansion ROM a simple matter of plugging in the new unit.) What do you need expansion ROM for? Expansion ROM is a form of *firmware,* as is the operating system. (*Firmware* – programs contained in a permanent medium, such as ROMs, and used to modify the operation of the computer. In the strictest sense firmware is a type of software. However, the programming is directed at the machine's operating system. Software is usually defined as programming that is loaded into RAM, and thus is temporary in nature, and is for the performance of some task for the user. A financial program on tape is software, a different language in ROM is firmware. (BASIC in your ROM comes with the computer, but is firmware.)) With expansion ROM, you can modify the operating system or the language of the computer without consuming any of the programmable RAM.

Additional functions, character sets, or languages can be implemented quickly and easily with expansion ROM. This can be very useful, but there is a tradeoff. Remember we only have 64K of potential memory locations. For every K that is reserved for expansion ROM, you lose a potential K of RAM. You can't have a block of memory locations serving both ROM and RAM. This is true whether you are using the expansion ROM or not. The space has been reserved. So you have to choose between expansion or a greater potential amount of RAM.

Size of ROM is somewhat meaningless, but the numbers game is important in RAM. RAM stores your programs and data. The more RAM, the longer your programs can be. Greater RAM also allows larger blocks of data to be entered in a machine. This can speed up data file manipulations. The machine can process data much faster when it can process (manipulate) data directly (while it's in RAM) as opposed to loading small pieces, processing, then

saving them back to tape or disk. Cassette tape drives move at a snail's pace compared to the speed of the computer working within its RAM. By loading an entire file into the RAM memory, you can proceed at *machine speeds* once the load is completed.

With a small RAM memory, you may be forced to load, process, load, process .... this can be tiresome. Larger RAM memories allow you to do more with your computer: write longer programs, and process faster. Another argument in favor of larger memories is the RAM requirements of commercially available software. Some programs *require* large memories. Most home applications programs will run on 8 or 16K, but there are some programs that require 32K or more depending on the model of the computer. (If you have more RAM than a program requires, it is no problem. However, if you attempt to run a program that exceeds the available RAM, the program will not run. The machine will *crash* (cease functioning) and display an error message indicating that you have run out of memory.)

What are the disadvantages? There is only one: cost. Extra RAM costs more. This does not mean that your order any amount of RAM that comes to mind. Models offer a certain amount of RAM and you choose which model you want.

How do you buy RAM? The available memories are almost as numerous as the machines. Some manufacturers offer the same basic machine with several choices of memory sizes (e.g. 8K, 16K, or 32K). Other manufacturers offer one model with a given amount which can be expanded, and offer a better model with more. Each manufacturer has his own way of doing this. You have to buy some definite amount, that is you can't order a "Data Cruncher Mark IV" with 19½K of RAM. You would have to buy either a 4K or a 16K or whatever "Data Crunchers" have available.

1, 2, 4, 5, 8, 16, 32, and 48K are the common amounts sold with computers. That represents a variety of machines, not one model. On some machines, with higher price tags, you may find 64K, 96K, 128K, 256K.

Another point about RAM. You can add additional RAM up to some maximum amount. That is, you can buy a computer with less than the ceiling on RAM, and add more RAM later up to that ceiling. The ceiling is defined by how many of the original 64K of memory locations are consumed by the operating system, the BASIC interpreter, and expansion ROM. If all of this added up to 16K, then the ceiling for RAM would be 48K.

What are the memory considerations? For RAM there are only two: 1. how much RAM do you need and can you afford on your initial purchase. 2. what is the maximum amount of RAM that the machine can handle, the ceiling mentioned above? A minimum of 8K is probably sufficient for most home applications. 16K should be more than sufficient, and possibly the best choice for a cost versus use consideration. Unless you have something quite specific in mind, perhaps you need not worry about getting more than 16K to begin with; you can always expand later. It depends entirely on your specific applications.

How do you decide on the amount of RAM you need? Define your applications, and then talk to experienced users and dealers. Also, if you will be using commercially available software, look into the RAM requirements of the software. You have to look at the overall machine. So integrate considerations on memory size into all of the advantages and disadvantages of the machine.

Screen Format *Screen format* describes the physical presentation of information on the screen of the video monitor or TV. The format is decided by the computer, not the video monitor. The monitor only displays what the computer tells it to. There are two terms which much be defined in order to understand screen formats: lines and columns.

Imagine that you have a typewriter in front of you. Insert a sheet of paper. Set the margins on both sides so that you can type 64 letters on one *line*. Starting on the left margin, type 64 X's. Don't return the carriage yet. Let's look at what you have right now. You have one *line* of X's. So a *line* is a group of *characters*

L	I	N	E	S	C	C	C	C	C
L	I	N	E	S	O	O	O	O	O
L	I	N	E	S	L	L	L	L	L
L	I	N	E	S	U	U	U	U	U
L	I	N	E	S	M	M	M	M	M
L	I	N	E	S	N	N	N	N	N
L	I	N	E	S	S	S	S	S	S

extending horizontally across the screen. (*Characters* — letters (ABC ...), numbers (123 ...), punctuation and symbols (,"#$), and graphic symbols are all characters. Any element that can be printed is a character. One

X	X	X	X	X	X	X	X	X	X
X	X	X	X	X	X	X	X	X	X
X	X	X	X	X	X	X	X	X	X
X	X	X	X	X	X	X	X	X	X

4 Lines, 10 Columns

letter is one character. The word *computer* contains 8 characters. The number 1981 contains 4 characters. Spaces or blanks are also considered characters.) More accurately, a *line* is the *space* on the sheet of paper that the characters are printed on. *Lines* exist whether anything is printed on them or not (e.g. a double-spaced, typed sheet has blank lines between the printed lines). So a *line* is the physical space extending horizontally across the sheet, or *screen*. OK, now how many X's did you type? 64. So we could say that you typed 64 characters per line. We could also say that your typewriter is adjusted to print 64 *columns*. *Columns* are simply the total number of possible characters per line. *Columns* extend vertically down the sheet of paper, or screen. Like lines, columns exist whether anything is printed in them or not.

Now, set the line spacing on your imaginary typewriter to single space. Return the carriage to the left margin, and type another 24 lines of X's, each line having 64 X's. You now have a rectangular block of X's. Go to the upper left hand corner of the block and count how many X's are printed across the sheet of paper. 64 right? Now, return to the upper left hand corner, and count how many X's are printed down the page along the left margin. 25. (The original line of X's plus 24 more lines.) If this were a video screen on a computer, we would say that the screen format for this particular computer is 64 columns by 25 lines.

The various computers on the market offer a variety of screen formats. Common column formats are 22, 24, 32, 40, 64, and 80 columns. Common line formats are 1 (hand-held computers), 16, 24, and 25. The more exotic machines may exceed these figures.

Why are screen formats important? The larger the format (the more lines and columns you have), the greater the amount of information you can display at one time. Let's consider four different formats: a hand-held with 26 columns by 1 line, a desk-top with 32 columns by 16 lines, a second desk-top with 40 columns by 25 lines, a third desk-top with 80 columns by 25 lines. These are all common formats. How many total characters can each format display?

Simply multiply the columns by the lines, thus we have 26 (1 X 26) for the hand-held, 512 (32 X 16) for the first desk-top, 1000 (40 X 25) for the second desk-top, and 2000 (80 X 25) for the third desk-top.

The more information that you can display at one time, the more useful and, unfortunately, the more expensive the computer is. The impact of screen format is determined by your main use for the computer. Again, you must balance cost against need.

Screen formats are fixed for each model. That is, you can't custom order any screen format for a particular model. Rather, you must find the model that has a screen format that you desire. Screen formats have to be factored into your selection process for the model that you will finally buy. Another feature that you may want is wrap-around. This is the ability to continue typing (a program) when you have reached the right margin on the screen, without using a carriage return. This is usually effective for two lines, sometimes three on the smaller machines. Essentially what happens is that when you reach the right side of the screen on the first line, rather than pressing return, you just keep typing. The text automatically advances one step and returns to the left side of the screen on the next line down. At the end of the second line, you must press return to continue. On the third line the text will wrap around again, and on the fourth you must press return.

It *is* important. Without going into detail, wrap-around allows twice as many characters of instructions to a line number. This can be an important memory-saving technique in programming. Another advantage is that peripherals are presented with a larger line length. Suppose that you have a 40 column screen display. With two-line wrap-around, the printer would see an 80 column line. Thus the computer acts like an 80 column machine, except for the video display. Wrap-around can be valuable.

Related to screen format is the *character matrix*. The character matrix is a block of Picture Elements, pixels, which is used to form the individual characters on the screen. Each pixel is like a light bulb, it may be on or off independently of the rest of the matrix. The matrix resembles a bank of light bulbs used on a scoreboard, or a time/temperature sign. By illuminating the proper pixels, any character (alphanumeric, graphics, punctuation, or symbols) can be displayed. For a period (.), only one pixel would need to be illuminated. For a flashing square, all of the pixels in the matrix would be illuminated, then off, then illuminated ....

The number of pixels in the character matrix is always given in terms of a horizontal dimension, and a vertical dimension. Common dimensions for a character matrix are: 5 X 7, 7 X 9, and 8 X 8. In 5 X 7, the character matrix has a dimension of 5 pixels horizontally, and 7 pixels vertically. The total number of pixels in the matrix is the product of the horizontal

A 5×7 "g"

A 5×9 "g"

and vertical dimensions (e.g. 35 for the 5 X 7). The larger matrices provide a finer *font*. (*Font* – style and size of any form of printing.) The lowercase letters can have true "descenders" for the letters g, j, p, q, and y. Descenders are the portion of these letters that *descend* below the bottom line established by the remaining letters.

A 5 X 7 matrix cannot produce descenders due to the short vertical dimension of the matrix. Letters without descenders have an elevated appearance, and the font is coarse and harder to read. The larger the character matrix dimensions (i.e. the more pixels in the matrix), the more detailed the font can be. The display will have a better appearance.

If we consider both screen format and the character matrix together, we come up with another specification: *maximum screen resolution*. This specification has a number of different names: resolution, maximum density, bit map .... All of these terms answer the same question: how many total pixels are available on the screen? Like the character matrix (and screen format), maximum screen resolution is given in horizontal and vertical dimensions. The horizontal dimension tells you how many pixels exist across the screen. It is simply the product of the number of horizontal pixels in the character matrix times the number of columns on the screen. The vertical dimension tells you how many pixels exist vertically. It is the product of the number of vertical pixels in the character matrix times the number of lines on the screen. The total number of pixels on the screen is the product of the horizontal dimension times the vertical dimension.

Let's consider a computer that has 64 columns, 25 lines, and a 7 X 9 character matrix. The maximum resolution would be 448 X 225 (64 X 7 = 448 and 25 X 9 = 225). We would have a total of 448 pixels across the screen, and 225 pixels down the screen. The total number of pixels on the screen is 100,800 (448 X 225 = 100,800). What is the importance of maximum screen resolution? It states how many pixels you can control with high-resolution graphics. Otherwise, it is an interesting specification for trivia fans. Regarding high resolution graphics, you want big numbers, the bigger the better. The more pixels you have, the more you can do with high resolution graphics. We will discuss this further when we describe graphics.

All of these screen considerations are fixed by the manufacturer. The only choice you have in the matter is picking the best model to fit your requirements. You can't custom order a particular screen format.

Keyboards The keyboard is not really part of the computer. It is an input peripheral. Due to the fact that most models of computers have a keyboard included, we will take a look at some of the aspects of a keyboard. Don't underestimate the importance of a keyboard. You will be spending hours pounding away on it so it is a critical consideration. You will often see the term *human engineering* used in relation to keyboards. Human engineering is the concept of designing something that is practical and comfortable for human beings to use. You can have the most wonderfully designed keyboard in terms of electronics and, if it is uncomfortable to use, it's not worth buying. Shop for human engineering in keyboards.

Some models offer a detachable keyboard. The keyboard is a separate unit from the computer and, generally, is not larger than the area required for the keys. This is a nice feature in that it allows some freedom of movement independent of the computer and the video monitor. You can adjust the keyboard placement for the most comfort quite easily. Also you can move the board out of your work area when it is not in use.

Another area you should investigate is the layout of the keyboard. We have not seen, as yet, anything offered other than *QWERTY* keyboard on computers. (*QWERTY Keyboard* – the standard layout for a typewriter keyboard, named after the arrangement of the letters in the top row of letters: *QWERTYUIOP.* QWERTY was designed to reduce hammer jams in the early model typewriters, and human engineering was not considered. QWERTY is criticized for being difficult to use, and hard to learn.) However, the idea of dropping QWERTY for something better is being discussed. For now, though, it appears that we are stuck with QWERTY.

Some manufacturers place all of the numbers and, in some units, the arithmetic operators (+, -, *, /) in a calculator-like keypad to the right of the main keyboard. (BASIC uses the * to denote multiplication, and the / to denote division.) This layout has two advantages: 1. the numerical keypad is very convenient for math operations. 2. additional characters can be added to the empty keys normally used for the numbers and the shifted position of the extra numerical keys. The only disadvantage is that the keyboard has to be somewhat larger.

Also notice the location of special function keys, especially those that may have a devastating result if inadvertently struck (RESET key). Any command keys should be located so that it is difficult to accidentally strike them during normal use.

There are several types of keyboard construction. The two major categories are the flat panel, touch sensitive (membrane), and the mechanical switch (or contact) types. The flat panel can use the same layout, and can perform the same functions as any other keyboard. The keyboard is flat; there are no bumpy individual keys sticking up. Key placement is indicated by labeled blocks printed on a plastic sheet, which is glued or laminated to the surface of the board. The flat panel has the appearance of a diagram of a keyboard that one might find in an instruction manual. It is wafer thin, very light, cheap to manufacture, and, with no moving parts, it is very rugged. Flat panel keyboards are being used extensively by industry in hostile environments. Since it is flat, it is very easy to clean. The flat panel keyboard is less sensitive to peanut butter, jam, candy, soft drinks, and abusive pounding. It can be a wise choice for children.

With all of these advantages, you may wonder why the computer industry has relegated the flat panel to the low cost models only. There is no tactile feedback with a flat panel keyboard. You cannot feel the locations of the keys, nor can you feel a response to a keystroke. There *is* no keystroke. Typing on a flat panel keyboard is like typing on the top of a desk. Touch typists have nothing to touch; there is no feeling that the key has been actuated. So, for all of its advantages, which are considerable, the flat panel's failure to involve our sense of touch is its great weakness.

Everything that is advantageous about the flat panel is a disadvantage with the mechanical switch type. They are expensive, delicate, and difficult to clean. They use contacts which oxidize and get dirty. They cannot be used in hostile environments or by hostile people. Liquids and humidity are murderous to them. Because they have moving parts, they can wear out.

Chances are good that the keyboard could cause more maintenance problems than anything else in the computer.

With all of these disadvantages, the mechanical switch keyboard has its one very big advantage: you can feel the keys. You don't have to keep one eye on the keyboard (if you touch type). You can feel the key's response and know that the character has been entered.

Within the mechanical switch category, there are a variety of stroke depths, key sizes, and stroke pressures. Sizes range from tiny, on the hand-helds, to what is known as the full-size keyboard. The full-size is similar to a standard typewriter keyboard. Stroke depth (the distance the key travels during the stroke) and stroke pressure (the force required to strike a key) vary on the different models. Generally, an expensive keyboard will have a very positive response; a light, but even pressure and, perhaps, a slight snapping action at the bottom of the stroke called a detent. Cheap keyboards will usually have a very shallow stroke depth and a "mushy" feel. The feel of a keyboard, of course, is a very subjective matter. Your best test of a keyboard is to try it out.

A feature that you want on any keyboard is two or three key *rollover*. This is the ability of the keyboard to distinguish small nuances in time passing between two keys being struck almost simultaneously, and to keep the order correct. Without rollover, touch typists would have a terrible time with characters getting out of order or lost altogether. You want rollover.

You don't want *bounce*. Keyboard or switch bounce is the multiple entry of a character when only one character was desired (sswwiittcchh bboouunnccee). Keyboard bounce is caused by microscopic bouncing of the contacts during a keystroke. All mechanical switches have switch bounce, but special circuitry is implemented to eliminate the effect. However, a bad keyboard can overcome the circuitry and, on occasion, a character may be entered more than once. Keyboard bounce can be lived with, if it is not excessive, but it is always aggravating. Naturally, a manufacturer is not going to advertise that their computer has a bounce, so you have to ask experienced users or dealers about the problem. Get a number of opinions; people have been known to hint about bounce on a particular model they don't like. It's like saying a particular car has transmission trouble; it may or may not be true.

If you can touch type, or you intend to do a lot of programming, or you intend to use the computer for word processing, you need a good quality, mechanical switch type of keyboard. If the computer will be used mainly by young children, a flat panel, touch sensitive keyboard might be best. If you will be doing a lot of numerical work, look into a model with a separate numerical keypad.

Unfortunately, you don't get much of a choice on keyboards either. Don't underestimate the importance of a keyboard. It is your primary method of communicating with the computer.

Graphics And Character Sets Graphics are computer-generated illustrations and graphs. In essence, any nonverbal and non-numerical information is considered graphics. There are two general categories: low resolution and high resolution. Most home computers feature graphics, some models are limited to low resolution.

With low resolution graphics, the machine will have a given number of standard graphic characters. These characters are internally generated in the same manner as the alphanumeric characters. Each character is assigned a key on the keyboard, usually in the shifted mode, and they are typed or programmed on the screen in the same fashion as alphanumeric characters.

When using low resolution graphics, the only decisions you have are which character you want and at what location on the screen you want it. Because the characters are internally generated, you cannot modify them to meet your exact requirements. Lines are usually limited to verticals, horizontals, and diagonals. Curves are very crude, if not impossible. As a result, low resolution graphics lack detail and have a "blocky" appearance.

High resolution graphics illuminate the individual pixels of the character matrix anywhere on the screen. You can make very detailed drawings as the screen becomes a giant matrix of thousands of individual dots which can be illuminated independently of one another. You can draw curves, irregular angles, three dimensional figures, and those fascinating geometrical constructions which are graphic representations of mathematical functions. As a comparison, imagine two artists painting a picture. One uses a fine set of art brushes (high resolution), the other uses a two inch house brush (low resolution).

If your interest is in low resolution graphics, look for the greatest number of different characters and the largest screen format. This will give you a greater versatility and allow a more detailed image. If high resolution interests you, you want to look for the largest maximum screen resolution. You want many pixels: the more, the better. The number of pixels will determine the detail of your image. High resolution graphics are somewhat more expensive. Some machines have high resolution graphics as a standard feature. Others offer it as an option, and some models rely on add-on boards offered by separate, specialty manufacturers. If you are especially interested in computer graphics, you will want high resolution graphics. If you cannot afford them initially, make sure that the machine of your choice can be expanded to include them.

The *character set* is the total package of characters that can be displayed on the screen. The character set includes alphanumeric, symbols and punctuation, graphics, and special notation (e.g. mathematical notation, Greek letters for engineering, special punctuation used in foreign languages). Character sets differ from machine to machine, and, to some degree, are an indicator of price. The very low cost units may offer only uppercase letters, the minimum of punctuation and symbols, numbers, and perhaps a smattering of graphic characters. However, in many cases, additional specialized symbols can be added to the machine with firmware.

Related to the character set are special video effects. The most common is reverse video. In normal video, the character is illuminated on a black

background. The only portion of the character matrix that is illuminated is that portion which is required to form the character. In reverse video, the character is black and the remainder of the character matrix is illuminated. If you had one word printed in reverse video on an otherwise blank screen, you would see a black screen with an illuminated stripe (one line high and the same length as the word), with the word printed in black letters on the stripe. Other special effects include flashing and underlining.

For general home use, all you really need are the uppercase letters, standard punctuation and symbols, numbers, and some graphic characters. In fact, a greater variety of graphics may be more useful to you than lowercase letters. However, if you think that you will be word processing, you'll want lowercase letters. If you have a specialized use (e.g. higher math, engineering), find a machine which will either accommodate your needs as is, or has the necessary firmware available.

Languages Most of the desk-top computers offer BASIC (*B*eginners *A*ll-purpose *S*ymbolic *I*nstruction *C*ode). Unfortunately, each manufacturer has its own version of BASIC, and, in some cases, newer models may have a revised BASIC which differs from the older models.

Selecting a computer on the basis of language is a tough job for anyone, but for the beginner it is even more difficult. Each machine may have 50 or more different commands and functions, some of which can be found on all of the machines, and others which are exclusive to a particular machine. Some of the functions are the same, but named differently. A machine may appear not to have a certain function when actually it does, but it implements the function in a different manner.

Your best bet is to contact experienced microcomputer users and dealers for this. For you to investigate all of the functions on all of the machines is a timeless undertaking. When you also don't know what half of the functions are used for, it becomes impossible. Another source is magazine reviews. A review will usually pinpoint the strengths and weaknesses of the language used on the machine.

None of the established computers have a terrible BASIC; don't lose sleep worrying about it. If your use is general home applications, just about any BASIC will likely be good enough. If you have a specialized use, one machine may have a better version of BASIC for your application, but most of the machines can be programmed to get around any deficiencies. The exception to the above, are some of the very low priced units. You may find some serious limitations in the language. If you are considering one of these units, study the BASIC offered.

PASCAL, FORTH, and PILOT are gaining popularity as alternatives to BASIC. You may want to write programs "in" them sometime. Some models even have FORTRAN available. If you are interested in programming, look into the languages available for your selected computer.

At times a high level language is too slow to perform a certain task. This is especially true for graphics used in *simulations,* in which the screen must be updated very rapidly. (*Simulations* – use of the computer to simulate real or fictional situations. Simulations are used extensively in games and educational programs.) The problem can be overcome by programming in machine language. A great amount of time is saved by eliminating the interpretation of a high level language into machine language, the only language that the processor understands.

Graphic functions, which may take several seconds to execute in BASIC, can be performed in a few milliseconds (one thousandth of a second) in machine language. Due to the fact that this speed is much faster than the visual response of the eye, machine language graphics can appear real. Some machines have assembly language, which is simply machine language programmed in alphabetic abbreviations called *mnemonics.* (*mnemonics* – (ne moni ks) aids to the memory.) The mnemonics are much easier for for humans to learn and remember than hexidecimal codes (e.g. "load the accumulator" is A9 in "hex," but its mnemonic is "LDA" on the 6502 microprocessor.) Machine language and assembly language achieve the same goal: extremely rapid program execution implemented by talking to the processor in its own language. By learning machine language, you can discover much about the hardware concepts of your computer and the way computers, in general, work.

Color Do you need color? The answer can only be determined by you. It is debatable that you need color, but it does add to games, graphs, etc. Can you afford color? Don't forget that, with color, you must pay more for your display. Some monochrome (one color, generally black and white or green and white display) models have their display already built in. So don't forget the price of the display when making your pricing comparisons. A color TV or monitor can be as expensive as the computer itself.

Where is color most useful? For games and educational programs. Educational programs, especially for younger children, are enhanced with color. Creative programming with color can be very conducive to maintaining attention. Another primary use of color is in graphics (using the computer to form images). Imagery is much more interesting to the eye in color. If one of your principal interests is computer graphics, the color machine becomes even more necessary. Color is less important in financial, word and information processing, unless you're interested in the more expensive systems that can generate color graphs and charts.

Assuming that you do want color, what should you look for? First, realize that you don't get every color in the rainbow. Most models offer 8 or 16 basic colors. Some will allow you to perform various intensity and shading tricks, bringing your number of available shades up as high as 128 different "colors." Check the number of available hues. Another issue is the versatility of the color functions. How many colors can be displayed simultaneously on the screen? How easy is the color to work with? How accessible are color "commands" in the computer's programming language? If color is an important factor in your choice, then it should be versatile and easy to program. We have a tendency to think of computers as either color or monochrome, as we think of a TV. Remember that each computer is capable of a great number of different tasks, and each model has a distinct set of features and limitations. Color should only be one factor. You shouldn't make a pass/fail screening test to eliminate 50% of the machines right away. You want the best total package to fit your requirements. It all goes back to knowing what you're doing. Take your time, and personally evaluate your options.

Software If you have a specific job in mind, software availability may make the difference between a useful machine and a dust collector. For the general home user, there is a myriad of programs to choose from. The software ranges from backgammon to recipe costs, arithmetic for children to energy conservation calculations, etc. Think of any subject and chances are that someone is selling a program related to it.

Some models of computers have a great amount of commercially available software. Others, for some reason, do not. Also, some software is available only for certain machines. If you will be dependent on commercially available software, (doing no programming yourself), choose a model with a large selection. Bear in mind however, that a recently introduced model will be lacking in software. Over time, software will be written for it.

A related consideration is the availability of firmware. One nice thing about firmware is that you can change the manner in which the computer operates without consuming any useable RAM, and you don't have to load a program to implement the change.

You can find a lot of information about software availability in magazine advertisements. One thing to realize is that, in most cases, independent software houses will offer more software for a particular

machine than does the manufacturer of the machine.
Look beyond what the manufacturer offers. Dealers
are also a good source of information on software
availability. There are some software directories
available and many dealers have these on hand.

A word of caution: after you get your computer,
choose your software carefully. Due to abuses of
copyrighted software, dealers are becoming reluctant
to refund or exchange purchased software.

Documentation *Documentation* refers to the
instruction manuals, programming manuals, theory
of operation, and trouble-shooting information
provided with the computer. Good documentation is
essential. Your understanding and the ultimate
usefulness of the computer depend on the quality of
the documentation. Some documentation is excellent;
most is adequate. Fortunately, when a manufacturer
provides poor documentation someone will usually
write a book on the machine. Sometimes, you can
purchase the instruction manuals separately.

Peripherals Do you need peripherals? Yes, unless
you only intend to use the computer as a space heater.
Peripherals communicate with the computer.

We think of a computer as being a box with a
keyboard and TV sitting on it. Actually, we have a
computing system: the computer, an input peripheral
(the keyboard), and an output peripheral (the TV or
video monitor). If any one of the three items fails, the
whole system becomes useless. If all three items are
installed on a common chassis, you should still
visualize them as a computer with two peripherals.
You will be buying some peripherals whether you
realize it or not.

What other peripherals do you need? It depends.
Specialized uses require specialized peripherals (a
printer for word processing). As a general statement,
the more peripherals you have in a system, the more
useful the system will be.

Buy peripherals as you need (and can afford) them. 1. If you decide that computing is not really for you, there is less equipment to sell off at a depreciated price. 2. You, as a beginner, have enough to learn for a while with the purchase of a minimal system. 3. After you have used your system and have become familiar with computing, you may redefine your needs. When you have some experience, you will be better able to make decisions on peripherals.

On the other hand, you might be offered a significant price cut in a package deal. Otherwise, you should buy a good minimum system. But don't cut corners on your basic system in order to throw in that flashy extra item. A good minimum system has far more potential than an ill-planned extensive system.

You may also want to consider joysticks, game paddles, or a light pen since these items are rather inexpensive ($20 to $50 per item). They can add to the pleasure of playing games.

When shopping for a computer, you want to look for standard I/O (Input/Output) ports. An I/O port

connects the computer to the peripherals and, while this may seem simple, it is actually quite complex. The processor and the peripherals talk back and forth, "shake hands," and all sorts of timing issues are involved.

There are two general categories of I/O ports used by the manufacturers: standard and nonstandard. Standard ports use an accepted convention for signal levels and wiring connectors. Nonstandard ports can seem the result of whimsy. Nonstandard ports are rather like selling a car with 14½ inch wheels. They work, but where do you buy tires? Peripherals made by the same manufacturer always connect up with no problem. But peripherals made by other manufacturers and wired for standard ports will not work unless interface circuitry is added. Some of the interfacing required can get expensive and the more you have in a signal path, the greater the likelihood of trouble.

There are two primary standard ports: RS-232C, and the IEEE 488. The RS-232C is the most popular and is a serial port. That is, the information is transferred one bit at a time. The IEEE 488 is a parallel port; 8 bits or one word is transferred at a time. The advantage of using standardized ports is that the computer is compatible with any peripheral which is designed for that port. Thus an RS-232C peripheral will work on any computer with an RS-232C port, regardless of manufacturer. The same is true for the IEEE 488. This gives you a greater selection of peripherals from which to choose. Some machines have standard ports (electronically), but use nonstandard connectors. This is a minor inconvenience, and is easily solved by an adapter cable.

One last word on peripherals. When buying a peripheral or, for that matter, a computer, try to get a feeling for how stable the manufacturer is. It would be discouraging to sink your money into a device, and then see the manufacturer fold up. Spare parts become unavailable, and the equipment can gradually become worthless. This is especially true for mechanical devices such as printers. Mechanical parts wear out. You may get a better price on off brands, but is it worth the risk of not being able to repair your machine?

Bringing It Home

You have probably given a lot of thought to which machine you want and what you are going to do with it, but have you considered where will you put the computer? While the *computer* may not seem to be all that big, it's amazing how much space *computing* requires. Also, the computer, an electronic device, is somewhat finicky about its environment. Finding a suitable location with enough space can be a problem.

Let's consider location. Heat and humidity are unpleasant to computers. So don't place the computer in front of a heater duct, and keep it out of the humid areas of your home. That probably eliminates 95% of the basements in the world. You also have to watch out for rooms that are located close to kitchens, bathrooms, or laundry rooms; any area that generates a lot of humidity is not good. You also want to be somewhat isolated from general living areas. A computer does not like people crashing into it, nor

gooey-fingered kids. If you intend to program the computer, you will need a quiet area. Scratch the living room, family room, and game room.

Your location will need a lot of space, several electrical outlets, and good lighting. Summing up, you need a cool, dry, quiet, isolated room with lots of space, lighting, and outlets.

What do you need in the way of space? This discussion will assume that you will be doing some programming. You need an table top that will accommodate the computer, all of the peripherals, workspace for writing, and space for reference materials.

Both sides of the keyboard should have room for several books and magazines as well as your own notes. You will need bookshelves for your documentation, reference books, magazines, and personal notes. (All of this will accumulate at an amazing rate.) Storage space that is free from magnetic fields (e.g. motors, electronic gear, magnets, tools with magnetic tips, even house wiring) is required for tapes and disks. (Please note that a wooden drawer does not offer any protection against magnetic fields. Distance, and a steel (not aluminum or other non-ferrous material) container are the only protection against magnetic fields.) Proper storage of your magnetic media is important, as contact with a magnetic field can destroy hours of programming, an expensive software package, or important data files.

You will need several electrical outlets. You will need a receptacle for the computer and some peripherals (some peripherals can draw power from the computer). Also, you may need some receptacles for lamps, clocks, and other appliances, and you should always have a spare outlet for temporary equipment (e.g. soldering iron, demagnetizer, etc.). (*demagnetizer* – an electromagnet used to remove the magnetic field that builds up on tape heads through normal use.)

If you don't have enough outlets available, have

them installed rather than stringing extension cords
all over the place. You may want to throw in a few
extras for future expansion. Another thing to look at
is the type of receptacle installed in your location. If
you have an older home, your outlets may be the old,
two-prong type. This type of outlet will not
accommodate grounded plugs (three-prong) or
polarized plugs (two-prong, one larger than the other).
If your equipment has either of the above plugs, you
will not be able to use your outlets. Don't modify the
plug to match the outlet, rather, replace the outlet. The
manufacturers use those plugs for some very good
reasons; your safety, radio frequency interference
suppression, and internal noise suppression. (*Radio
Frequency Interference* — interference to radio and TV
reception caused by the high frequency square wave
timing (clock) pulses generated by the computer. *Noise*
— unwanted signal variations caused by external
interference, line voltage variations, or internal signal
leakage. The computer can misinterpret noise for a
valid signal, and function improperly as a result.) You
should avoid defeating the engineering that went into
your computer.

Another item you may want at your location is a
phone line. If you intend to use an information network
such as The Source, or Micronet or to talk to another
computer via the phone, you will need a phone line for
the communication medium. If you will be using an
acoustically coupled modem, be sure to have a phone
with a standard handset. (*Modem* — (*modulator/
demodulator*) a device for the conversion of computer
signals into signals which are compatible with
telephone lines, and vice versa. Modems are used to
connect computers together over any distance in which
conventional wiring is impractical or uneconomical.
An acoustically coupled modem converts the computer
signal into audible "beeps." The "beeps" are fed into a
standard telephone by placing the handset into
acoustic cups on the modem. Seals prevent interference

from external noise, and are similar to the ear cushions on a stereo headset. The handset transmits the "beeps" in the form of normal phone signals. Also, the modem receives "beeps" from the handset and converts them into computer signals. Direct-connect modems function in the same manner, except the computer signal is converted to the phone signal with no audible "beeps." They are *directly connected* to the phone line.) Early French or designer phones do not seal in the acoustic cups very well.

While we are on the subject of your home, don't neglect insurance. Call your agent and make sure that the computer will be covered for fire, theft, acts of God, etc.

Give some thought and consideration to your location and utilization of space. Your layout should be designed around your application. For instance, a computer used primarily for games would be located and set up entirely different than one used for word processing. Consider future expansion. It would be nice to be able to add a peripheral without throwing the entire layout into upheaval.

Frequently used items should be in easy reach and allow sufficient work space for writing. If you lack furniture for the placement of your system, you can buy desks that are customized to the exact machine for the popular models.

Have we covered everything? Hardly. What about tone generators? Some computers offer them as standard equipment. With a tone generator, you can add noise to your games, audible prompting to your programs, or compose music. The S-100 bus? It's a family of circuit board components all using a common wiring scheme (the scheme is the *S-100 bus*). This system allows a high degree of flexibility because the user creates his own computer by selecting specific circuit boards to meet his or her needs.

What about CP/M? CP/M (*Control Program for Microcomputers*) is an operating system found on the high cost units (higher cost in terms of home computers; cost is a relative term, highly dependent on the environment in consideration). CP/M is something of an industry standard so it has a large software base.

This booklet is not a comprehensive course in computers. It is a starting place, the beginning of a path up the mountain of information about computing. If we have given you some direction and a few definitions, we will consider it successful.

Specification Chart Information and Analysis:
On the pages that follow, you'll find a series of charts providing you with detailed information about most of the major personal computers on the market today. We'll use one as an example to help you apply the information learned in Part III.

Charts And Analysis

MEMORY

	RAM Standard:	Expansion to:	ROM Expansion
Apple IIe	64K	128K	Cards
Atari 400	16K	48K	Cartridges
Atari 800	48K	48K	Cartridges
Atari 1200XL	64K	64K	Cartridges
Atari "My First Computer"	8K	32K	Cartridges
Commodore 64	64K	64K	Cartridges
Commodore 128	128K	896K	Cartridges
Commodore B Series	128K	896K	Cartridges
Commodore BX Series	256K	896K	Cartridges
Commodore HHC-4 (hand-held)	4K	16K	Packs
Commodore Executive 64	64K	64K	Cartridges
Commodore PET/CBM	32K	96K	Internal sockets
Commodore Super PET	96K	96K	Internal sockets
Commodore VIC-20	5K	32K	Cartridges
Epson HX-20 Notebook Computer	16K	32K	Cartridges
IBM Personal Computer	16K	512K	Cards
Kaypro II	64K	64K	—
Mattel Aquarius	4K	52K	Cartridges
Mattel Intellivision Computer System	N/A	N/A	Cartridges

Charts And Analysis

	RAM Standard:	Expansion to:	ROM Expansion
NEC PC-6001	16K	32K	Cartridges
NEC PC-8001A	32K	160K	One internal socket
Osborne I	64K	64K	—
Panasonic Hand-held Computer	2K	8K	Capsules
Panasonic JR-200U	32K	32K	Cartridges
Radio Shack Color Computer	16K	32K	Program "Paks"
Radio Shack Pocket Computer (PC II)	1.85K	16K	—
Radio Shack TRS 80 III	16K	48K	—
Spectravideo SV-318	16K	128K	Cartridges
Spectravideo SV-328*	64K	128K	Cartridges
TI-99/2	4.2K	36.2K	Cartridges
TI-99/4A	16K	48K	Cartridges
TI Compact Computer 40 (hand-held)	6K	16K	Plug-in port
Timex Sinclair TS-1000	2K	64K	Cartridges
Timex Sinclair TS-2000	16K	48K	Cartridges
Video Technology VZ-200	4K	64K	Cartridges

*These are tentative manufacturer's specifications.

MASS MEMORY STORAGE

	Tape Drive	Disk Drive
Apple IIe	X	Up to six
Atari 400	X	Up to four floppy disks (92K)
Atari 800	X	Same as 400
Atari 1200XL	X	Same as 400
Atari "My First Computer"	X	
Commodore 64	X	Up to five floppy disks (170K)
Commodore 128	X	Up to five floppy disks (160K)
Commodore B Series		Two built-in disk drives
Commodore BX Series		Two built-in disk drives
Commodore HHC-4 (hand-held)	X	
Commodore Executive 64		One or two built-in disk drives (170K)
Commodore PET/CBM	X	Up to four dual drives 340K or one MB dual density
Commodore Super PET	X	Same as PET/CBM
Commodore VIC-20	X	Up to five floppy disks (170K)
Epson HX-20 Notebook Computer	X	Optional floppy disks
IBM Personal Computer	X	Up to two disk drives (320K total)
Kaypro II		Two built-in disk drives
Mattel Aquarius	X	
Mattel Intellivision Computer System	X	

	Tape Drive	Disk Drive
NEC PC-6001	X	
NEC PC-8001A	X	Up to four disk drives (160K)
Osborne I		Built-in dual disk drives (100K)
Panasonic Hand-held Computer	(Up to 8K non-volatile RAM capsules)	
Panasonic JR-200U	X	
Radio Shack Color Computer	X	Up to four disk drives (156K)
Radio Shack Pocket Computer (PC II)	X	
Radio Shack TRS 80 III	X	Up to four disk drives (175K)
Spectravideo SV-318	X	Optional floppy disks
Spectravideo SV-328*	X	Optional floppy disks
TI-99/2	X	
TI-99/4A	X	Optional floppy disks
TI Compact Computer 40 (hand-held)	X	
Timex Sinclair TS-1000	X	
Timex Sinclair TS-2000	X	
Video Technology VZ-200	X	

Charts And Analysis

KEYBOARD

	Keyboard Type	Total Keys	Function Keys	Numeric Keypad
Apple IIe	Full stroke	63	2	No (optional plug-in avail.)
Atari 400	Membrane	61	3	No (optional plug-in avail.)
Atari 800	Full stroke	61	3	No (optional plug-in avail.)
Atari 1200XL	Full stroke	54	4	No
Atari "My First Computer"	Moving rubber key	56	0	No
Commodore 64	Full stroke	66	4	No
Commodore 128	Full stroke	94	10	Yes
Commodore B Series	Full stroke	94	10	Yes
Commodore BX Series	Full stroke	94	10	Yes
Commodore HHC-4 (hand-held)	Calculator style	40	0	Yes
Commodore Executive 64	Full stroke	66	4	No
Commodore PET/CBM	Full stroke	73	0	Yes
Commodore Super PET	Full stroke	73	0	Yes
Commodore VIC-20	Full stroke	66	4	No
Epson HX-20 Notebook Computer	Full stroke	68	5	No
IBM Personal Computer	Full stroke	83	10	Yes
Kaypro II	Full stroke	72	20	Yes
Mattel Aquarius	Moving rubber key	49	0	No
Mattel Intellivision Computer System	Full stroke	49	0	No

	Keyboard Type	Total Keys	Function Keys	Numeric Keypad
NEC PC-6001	Full stroke	71	5	No
NEC PC-8001A	Full stroke	82	5	Yes
Osborne I	Full stroke	69	14	Yes
Panasonic Hand-held Computer	Full stroke	65	5	No
Panasonic JR-200U	Moving rubber key	63	0	No
Radio Shack Color Computer	Calculator style	53	4	No
Radio Shack Pocket Computer (PC II)	Calculator style	66	8	Yes
Radio Shack TRS 80 III	Full stroke	65	4	Yes
Spectravideo SV-318	Moving rubber key	71	10	No
Spectravideo SV-328	Full stroke	71	10	Yes
TI-99/2	Moving rubber key	48	0	No
TI-99/4A	Full stroke	48	0	No
TI Compact Computer 40 (hand-held)	Calculator style	43	0	Yes
Timex Sinclair TS-1000	Flat membrane	40	0	No
Timex Sinclair TS-2000	Moving rubber key	40	0	No
Video Technology VZ-200	Moving rubber key	45	0	No

SCREEN FORMAT

	Lines x Characters	Highest Possible Resolution	Character Matrix	Upper- and Lowercase
Apple IIe	24 x 40	280h x 192v	5 x 7	Yes
Atari 400	24 x 40	320h x 192v	8 x 8	Yes
Atari 800	24 x 40	320h x 192v	8 x 8	Yes
Atari 1200XL	24 x 40	320h x 192v	8 x 8	Yes
Atari "My First Computer"	24 x 32	192h x 160v	—	Yes
Commodore 64	25 x 40	320h x 200v	8 x 8	Yes
Commodore 128	25 x 40	320h x 200v	8 x 8	Yes
Commodore B Series	25 x 80	320h x 200v	9 x 14	Yes
Commodore BX Series	25 x 80	320h x 200v	—	Yes
Commodore HHC-4 (hand-held)	Single-line, 24-character LCD	—	5 x 7	No
Commodore Executive 64	25 x 40	320h x 200v	8 x 8	Yes
Commodore PET/CBM	25 x 40	—	6 x 8	Yes
Commodore Super Pet	25 x 80	—	8 x 8	Yes
Commodore VIC-20	22 x 23	176h x 184v	8 x 8	Yes
Epson HX-20 Notebook Computer	4 x 20 (LCD)	120h x 32v	5 x 7	Yes
IBM Personal Computer	25 x 80	640h x 200v	9 x 9	Yes
Kaypro II	24 x 80	—	—	Yes
Mattel Aquarius	40 x 24	320h x 200v	—	Yes
Mattel Intellivision Computer System	20 x 12	160h x 192v	8 x 8	No

	Lines x Characters	Highest Possible Resolution	Character Matrix	Upper- and Lowercase
NEC PC-6001	16 x 32	256h x 192v	—	Yes
NEC PC-8001A	25 x 80	800h x 230v	7 x 9	Yes
Osborne I	24 x 52	364h x 240v	7 x 9	Yes
Panasonic Hand-held Computer	Single-line, 26 character LCD	159h x 8v	8 x 6	No
Panasonic JR-200U	24 x 32	64h x 48v	8 x 8	Yes
Radio Shack Color Computer	16 x 32	256h x 192v	6 x 16	No
Radio Shack Pocket Computer (PC II)	Single-line, 26-character LCD	156h x 7v	7 x 5	Yes
Radio Shack TRS 80 III	16 x 64	128h x 48v	6 x 8	Yes
Spectravideo SV-318	40 or 32 x 24	256h x 192v	—	Yes
Spectravideo SV-328	40 x 24	256h x 192v	—	Yes
TI-99/2	24 x 32	192h x 256v	—	No
TI-99/4A	24 x 32	192h x 256v	—	Yes*
TI Compact Computer 40 (hand-held)	Single-line, 31-character LCD	—	—	Yes
Timex Sinclair TS-1000	24 x 32	256h x 192v	—	No
Timex Sinclair TS-2000	24 x 32	256h x 192v	—	Yes
Video Technology VZ-200	16 x 32	128h x 64v	—	No

*"Lowercase" on the TI-99/4A is actually small caps.

COLOR AND GRAPHICS

	Color	Graphics Modes	Special Notes
Apple IIe	Yes	3	16 colors
Atari 400	Yes	14	Redefinable characters, 256 colors animation, special video chip
Atari 800	Yes	14	Same as 400
Atari 1200XL	Yes	14	Same as 400
Atari "My First Computer"	Yes	16	—
Commodore 64	Yes	4	16 colors, redefinable character set, animation with sprites
Commodore 128	Yes	4	Same as 64
Commodore B Series	No	—	—
Commodore BX Series	No	—	—
Commodore HHC-4 (hand-held)	No		
Commodore Executive 64	Yes	4	Same as 64
Commodore PET/CBM	No	1	Character graphics
Commodore Super PET	No	N/A	Special graphics characters
Commodore VIC-20	Yes	1	16 colors, special graphics characters, programmable character set
Epson HX-20 Notebook Computer	No	1	32 special graphics characters, dot-addressable graphics
IBM Personal Computer	Yes	2	16 colors in text mode, graphics characters, high resolution color and B/W graphics
Kaypro II	No	N/A	—
Mattel Aquarius	Yes	0	16 colors
Mattel Intellivision Computer System	Yes	0	16 colors

	Color	Graphics Modes	Special Notes
NEC PC-6001	Yes	3	Nine colors
NEC PC-8001A	Yes	2	Eight colors, Greek character set built in
Osborne I	No	1	32 graphics characters, 5-inch built-in B/W TV monitor
Panasonic Hand-held Computer	No	1	Optional TV interface allows 48 x 64, eight-color graphics
Panasonic JR-200U	Yes	1	Eight colors, 64 graphics symbols, 64 programmable characters
Radio Shack Color Computer	Yes	4	Extended color BASIC ROM kit adds graphic capabilities (optional)
Radio Shack Pocket Computer (PC II)	No	1	Dot addressable graphics
Radio Shack TRS 80 III	No	2	Special graphics character set
Spectravideo SV-318	Yes		16 colors, 52 graphics symbols, 32 sprites
Spectravideo SV-328	Yes		Same as SV-318
TI-99/2	No	1	
TI-99/4A	Yes	1	16 colors, 32 sprites, programmable characters
TI Compact Computer 40 (hand-held)	No	0	
Timex Sinclair TS-1000	No	1	Special graphics characters
Timex Sinclair TS-2000	Yes	1	Eight colors, FLASH command for blinking characters
Video Technology VZ-200	Yes	1	Eight color high resolution graphics

SOUND

	Available	Number of Voices
Apple IIe	Yes	One, internal speaker
Atari 400	Yes	Four
Atari 800	Yes	Four
Atari 1200XL	Yes	Four
Atari "My First Computer"	Yes	More than two
Commodore 64	Yes	Three; synthesizer
Commodore 128	Yes	Three; synthesizer
Commodore B Series	Yes	Three
Commodore BX Series	Yes	Three
Commodore HHC-4 (hand-held)	No	—
Commodore Executive 64	Yes	Three
Commodore PET/CBM	Yes	Built-in piezoelectric or add-on amplifier
Commodore Super PET	Yes	One
Commodore VIC-20	Yes	Three voices and one white noise generator
Epson HX-20 Notebook Computer	Yes	Four octaves with half-tones
IBM Personal Computer	Yes	One
Kaypro II	Yes (beeper)	One
Mattel Aquarius	Yes	One
Mattel Intellivision Computer System	No	—

	Available	Number of Voices
NEC PC-6001	Yes	Three voices with eight octave range plus noise generator
NEC PC-8001A	Yes	One
Osborne I	No	—
Panasonic Hand-held Computer	No	—
Panasonic JR-200U	Yes	Three voices, five octaves
Radio Shack Color Computer	Yes	One
Radio Shack Pocket Computer (PC II)	Yes	One
Radio Shack TRS 80 III	(Possible through cassette port)	One
Spectravideo SV-318	Yes	Three voices, eight octaves
Spectravideo SV-328	Yes	Three voices, eight octaves
TI-99/2	No	—
TI-99/4A	Yes	Three
TI Compact Computer 40 (hand-held)	No	—
Timex Sinclair TS-1000	No	—
Timex Sinclair TS-2000	Yes	One voice, ten octaves
Video Technology VZ-200	Yes	One

Charts And Analysis

LANGUAGES

	BASIC	PILOT	PASCAL	FORTRAN	FORTH	Other
Apple IIe	X	X	X	X	X	CP/M*, Compilers Logo, Assembler, Integer BASIC, BASIC A+
Atari 400	X	X	X		X	Assembler, Microsoft BASIC, Compilers, C/65
Atari 800	X	X	X		X	Same as 400
Atari 1200XL	X	X	X		X	Same as 400
Atari "My First Computer"	X					
Commodore 64	X				X	CP/M*, BASIC Compiler
Commodore 128	X		X	X		CP/M*, CP/M86*, COBOL, APL
Commodore B Series	X		X	X		Same as C128
Commodore BX Series	X		X	X		Same as C128
Commodore HHC-4 (hand-held)	X					
Commodore Executive 64	X					Same as C128
Commodore PET/CBM	X	X	X		X	Assembler, RPL COMAL, BASIC Compiler
Commodore Super PET	X		X	X	X	Assembler, APL, COBOL
Commodore VIC-20	X				X	Assembler, Extended BASIC
Epson HX-20 Notebook Computer	X					
IBM Personal Computer	X		X	X		Assembler, COBOL, other CP/M86 languages

	BASIC	PILOT	PASCAL	FORTRAN	FORTH	Other
Kaypro II	X					
Mattel Aquarius	X					
Mattel Intellivision Computer System	X					
NEC PC-6001	X					
NEC PC-8001A	X		X	X	X	C BASIC, COBOL
Osborne I	X		X	X		C BASIC, M BASIC, Assembler
Panasonic Hand-held Computer	X					SNAP
Panasonic JR-200U	X					
Radio Shack Color Computer	X					Logo, Assembler
Radio Shack Pocket Computer (PC II)	X					
Radio Shack TRS 80 III	X	X	X	X	X	COBOL, BASIC Compiler, CP/M
Spectravideo SV-318	X					
Spectravideo SV-328	X					
TI-99/2	X					
TI-99/4A	X		X			Extended BASIC, Logo
TI Compact Computer 40 (hand-held)	X					
Timex Sinclair TS-1000	X					
Timex Sinclair TS-2000	X					
Video Technology VZ-200	X					Microsoft BASIC

*CP/M and CP/M86 are registered trademarks of Digital Research, Inc.

Charts And Analysis

INTERFACES

	IEEE-488	RS-232C	Other
Apple IIe	X	X	
Atari 400	Proprietary serial port	Avail. as option	
Atari 800	Same as 400	Same as 400	
Atari 1200XL	Same as 400	Same as 400	
Atari "My First Computer"			
Commodore 64	Available as option	Requires adaptor	User port for modem, printer
Commodore 128	X	X	
Commodore B Series	X	X	
Commodore BX Series	X	X	
Commodore HHC-4 (hand-held)		X	
Commodore Executive 64		X	
Commodore PET/CBM	X		
Commodore Super PET	X	X	
Commodore VIC-20	Available as option	Requires adaptor	User port for modem, printer
Epson HX-20 Notebook Computer		X	40-pin connector
IBM Personal Computer		X	Modem card, parallel printer card
Kaypro II		X	
Mattel Aquarius		X	
Mattel Intellivision Computer System		X	

	IEEE-488	RS-232C	Other
NEC PC-6001			Centronics parallel
NEC PC-8001A			Centronics parallel, 50-pin data bus
Osborne I	X	X	Modem port
Panasonic Hand-held Computer			44-pin connector
Panasonic JR-200U		X	Centronics parallel
Radio Shack Color Computer		X	
Radio Shack Pocket Computer (PC II)			69-pin connector
Radio Shack TRS 80 III		X	
Spectravideo SV-318		X	
Spectravideo SV-328			
TI-99/2		Available as option	"Hex-Bus" interface included
TI-99/4A		Available as option	"Hex-Bus" interface optional
TI Compact Computer 40 (hand-held)		Available as option	"Hex-Bus" interface included
Timex Sinclair TS-1000			Expansion bus
Timex Sinclair TS-2000			Expansion bus
Video Technology VZ-200			Centronics-bus

TYPICAL STARTER SYSTEM

	Required Additional Devices*	Computer List Price†
Apple IIe	B/W or color TV	$1395
Atari 400	B/W or color TV Cassette recorder	under 250
Atari 800	B/W or color TV Cassette recorder	679
Atari 1200XL	B/W or color TV Cassette recorder	899
Atari "My First Computer"	B/W or color TV Cassette recorder	Less than 90
Commodore 64	B/W or color TV Cassette recorder	595
Commodore 128	B/W or color TV	795
Commodore B Series	—	1,695
Commodore BX Series	—	2,995
Commodore HHC-4 (hand-held)	—	199
Commodore Executive 64	—	995
Commodore PET/CBM	—	1495
Commodore Super PET	Disk drive	1995
Commodore VIC-20	B/W or color TV Datasette	199
Epson HX-20 Notebook Computer	—	795
IBM Personal Computer	B/W or color TV Cassette recorder	1,265
Kaypro II	No additional devices required. Built-in disk drive and CPT	1,795
Mattel Aquarius	B/W or color TV Cassette recorder	under 200
Mattel Intellivision Computer System	B/W or color TV Cassette recorder	under 200

Charts And Analysis

	Required Additional Devices*	Computer List Price†
NEC PC-6001	B/W or color TV Cassette recorder	$349
NEC PC-8001A	B/W or color TV	995
Osborne I	No additional devices required. Built-in disk drives and CRT	1795
Panasonic Hand-held Computer	—	under 500
Panasonic JR-200U	Cassette recorder	349
Radio Shack Color Computer	B/W or color TV Cassette recorder	299.95
Radio Shack Pocket Computer (PC II)	—	279.95
Radio Shack TRS 80 III	Cassette recorder	799
Spectravideo SV-318	B/W or color TV Cassette recorder	299
Spectravideo SV-328	B/W or color TV Cassette recorder	under 300
TI-99/2	B/W or color TV Cassette recorder	99.95
TI-99/4A	B/W or color TV Cassette recorder	under 300
TI Compact Computer 40 (hand-held)	—	249.95
Timex Sinclair TS-1000	B/W or color TV Cassette recorder	under 100
Timex Sinclair TS-2000	B/W or color TV Cassette recorder	149.95
Video Technology VZ-200	Cassette recorder	99

*To effectively use this system, these additional devices are necessary.
† This price does not include the cost of any required additional devices (such as TVs) listed above.

HIGHER LEVEL SYSTEM

	Added Peripherals
Apple IIe	Monitor, disk drive, 80-column text card
Atari 400	810 Disk Drive, modem, 16K additional memory
Atari 800	810 Disk Drive, modem, 16K additional memory
Atari 1200XL	Program recorder, 80-column dot-matrix printer, 40-column printer/plotter
Atari "My First Computer"	Printer, disk drive
Commodore 64	Video Pak, plug-in voice synthesizer, Digi-drum, VICmodem, color monitor
Commodore 128	
Commodore B Series	Single or dual floppy disks, dot-matrix and daisy wheel printers, modem
Commodore BX Series	Single or dual floppy disks, dot-matrix and daisy wheel printers, modem
Commodore HHC-4 (hand-held)	Interface module, which includes a small, built-in dot-matrix printer
Commodore Executive 64	Plug-in cartridge allowing use of CP/M
Commodore PET/CBM	"Winchester" hard disk drive, dual floppy disk drive.
Commodore Super PET	
Commodore VIC-20	Additional 16K RAM disk, color monitor, disk drive, VICmodem, dot-matrix printer, Digi-drum
Epson HX-20 Notebook Computer	Barcode reader, audio cassette, dot-matrix printer
IBM Personal Computer	Disk drive adapter 160K disk drive
Kaypro II	12-inch monitor
Mattel Aquarius	Mini-expander, printer, 4K or 16K memory cartridges, modem

	Added Peripherals
Mattel Intellivision Computer System	Music synthesizer, voice synthesizer, joystick controllers, system changer
NEC PC-6001	Expansion unit, disk drive, color monitor, printer
NEC PC-8001A	Expansion unit, disk drive, color monitor, printer, 32K additional memory
Osborne I	Video monitor Double density disk drives
Panasonic Hand-held Computer	
Panasonic JR-200U	Monitor, 80-column dot-matrix printer, modem
Radio Shack Color Computer	Disk drive Extended BASIC
Radio Shack Pocket Computer (PC II)	Combination printer and cassette interface with four-color printer/ plotter
Radio Shack TRS 80 III	Disk drive Additional 48K memory
Spectravideo SV-318	Dot-matrix printer, modem, seven-slot Super-Expander, disk drive, datasette
Spectravideo SV-328	Same as 318
TI-99/2	Four-color printer/plotter
TI-99/4A	Disk drive Additional 32K memory
TI Compact Computer 40 (hand-held)	Four-color printer/plotter wafer tape drive
Timex Sinclair TS-1000	32-column thermal printer 16K RAM pack
Timex Sinclair TS-2000	32-column thermal printer 16K RAM pack
Video Technology VZ-200	16K or 64K Memory Expansion Module

Manufacturers

Apple Computer, Inc.
20525 Mariana Ave.
Cupertino, CA 95014
(408) 996-1010

Atari, Inc.
1265 Borregas Ave.
Sunnyvale, CA 94086
(408) 745-2000

Commodore Business Machines
Consumer Products Division
487 Devon Park Dr.
Wayne, PA 19087
(215) 687-9750
Customer Support
(215) 687-4311

Epson
3415 Kashiwa St.
Torrance, CA 90505
(213) 539-9140

Hewlett Packard
Personal Computer Division
1000 N. E. Circle Blvd.
Corvallis, OR 97330
(503) 757-2000

IBM Corporation
National Marketing Center
Dept. 86-R
1133 Westchester Ave.
White Plains, NY 10604
(800) 431-2670

Kaypro
A Division of Non-Linear Systems
533 Stevens Ave.
Solana Beach, CA 92075
(619) 755-1134

Mattel Electronics
A Division of Mattel, Inc.
3600 Sepulveda Blvd.
Manhattan Beach, CA 90266
(213) 416-9169

Nippon Electric Co. Ltd. (NEC)
1401 Estes
Elk Grove Village, IL 60007
(312) 228-5900

Osborne Computer Corp.
26500 Corporate Ave.
Hayward, CA 94545
(415) 887-8080

The Panasonic Company
One Panasonic Way
Secaucus, NJ 07094
(201) 348-7000

Radio Shack
A Division of Tandy Corp.
1800 One Tandy Center
Fort Worth, TX 76102
(817) 390-3011

Sinclair Research
50 Stanford St.
Boston, MA 02114
(617) 742-4826

Spectravideo
39 W. 37th St.
New York, NY 10018
(212) 869-7911

Texas Instruments, Inc.
Consumer Relations
P.O. Box 53
(Attn: Accessories Dept.)
Lubbock, TX 79408
(806) 741-4800

Timex Computer Corp.
Waterbury, CT 06725
(800) 248-4639

Video Technology
2633 Greenleaf
Elk Grove Village, IL 60007
(312) 640-1776

Larger System Vendors

The following is a list of manufacturers not included in our comparison chart, whose computers are generally applicable to business and scientific environments.

ACT (Microsoft) Ltd.
FREEPOST
Birmingham B16 8BR
England

Applied Digital Data Systems
1000 Marcus Blvd.
Hauppauge, NY 11787
(516) 231-5400

Cromemco Inc.
280 Bernardo Ave.
Mountain View, CA 94040
(415) 964-7400

Data General Corporation
Westboro, MA 01581
(617) 366-8911

Digital Equipment Corp.
Parker Street, PK 3-2
Maynard, MA 01754
(617) 897-5111

Durango Systems
3003 North First Street
San Jose, CA 95134
(408) 946-5000

Intelligent Systems Corporation
Intecolor Drive
225 Technology Park
Atlanta, GA 30092
(404) 449-5961

Micro Technology, Unltd.
2806 Hillsborough St.
Raleigh, NC 27605
(919) 833-1458

North Star Computers Inc.
14440 Catalina St.
San Leandro, CA 94577
(415) 357-8500

Prodigy Systems Inc.
497 Lincoln Highway
Iselin, NJ 08830
(201) 283-2000

Smoke Signal Broadcasting
31336 Via Colinas
Westlake Village, CA 91362
(213) 889-9340

Vector Graphics
31364 Via Colinas
Westlake Village, CA 91362
(213) 991-2302

Glossary

BASIC Beginners All-purpose Symbolic Instruction Code. The language used in making programs which personal computers can follow. It contains about 50 words which can be rather easily learned. Other languages are also available, but the simplicity of BASIC and its similarities to ordinary English have made it the most popular.

BUS A group of lines, wires, or pins which carry computer data, timing, and control information to outside devices. Usually used to connect printers, disk drives, etc. to a computer.

BYTE A "cell" of computer memory, measured in groups of 1,024, called a *kilobyte*. 4K (4 kilobytes), 8K, and 16K are common amounts of RAM memory sold with consumer computers. More can usually be added later, but more is often unnecessary. A single byte could hold (remember) the letter "a."

CENTRONICS STANDARD An industry standard *parallel* interface used to attach a wide range of printers to computers.

CHARACTER MATRIX The "box" of pixels within which a screen text character is formed. Measured as vertical by horizontal dots, e.g. 8x8, 7x5, 9x9.

COMPUTER A machine which can follow instructions, manipulate information, and make decisions. A computer *thinks* (in some senses of the word). For example, today there are only a few hundred people in America who can win a game of chess against the best chess programs. It is predicted that, in a few years, a computer may become world chess champion, never to be beaten again by a human player.

CP/M (Control Program For Microcomputers) A popular *operating system* for microcomputers with Z80,8080, or similar MPUs. There is a huge amount of business software available that will run only with CP/M.

C.P.U. Central Processing Unit. This is the "brain" of a computer which interprets instructions and initiates actions.

CRT Cathode ray tube. Generally refers to any TV-like computer display.

CURSOR The indicator showing where the next typed character will appear on the screen, usually a white square.

CURSOR CONTROL The capability of moving the *cursor* horizontally or vertically to any point on the screen.

DATA Another word for information.

DISK DRIVE A mass-storage (large amount of memory) device which can be added to a computer to greatly increase the speed and amount of information manipulated at one time. This can become necessary if you are using your computer to keep business inventories or other immense collections of data. For nearly all personal applications, *floppy disks* are adequate. Looking like limp 45-rpm records, these disks can work together to bring up to one million bytes "on line" (available immediately) to whatever computer program is using them. At present, a floppy disk drive costs about the same as the computer it serves.

DUAL DRIVE   A disk drive consisting of two single floppy disk drives in the same unit. It can hold two diskettes simultaneously.

EXPANDABILITY   The capability of adding additional hardware to your computer such as more memory, color graphics, new languages in ROM, etc. Implemented through "expansion slots," "expansion ports," the S-100 bus, ROM sockets, cartridges, plug-in boards, or cards.

FUNCTION KEYS   Special keys that can perform commands at a touch of a button. *Cursor control* keys are function keys. Some computers have programmable, or user-definable function keys.

GAME PORT   Small parallel computer port that can be used to attach joysticks, paddles, and light pens.

GRAPHICS MODE/GRAPHICS SCREEN   A special display where individual dots can be illuminated to produce lines, curves, and drawings. Different modes vary in resolution, available colors, and amount of memory used.

HARD DISK   A high-performance, massive memory disk drive that uses a sealed, fixed disk surface which spins at a much greater speed than floppy disk drives. Advantage: huge storage capacity, 5-20 megabytes. Disadvantage: relatively high cost ($5,000 +).

IEEE-488   An IEEE (Institute of Electrical and Electronic Engineers) standard for attaching laboratory equipment to computers via a *parallel* interface. Used in some computers as a communications port (instead of RS-232, S-100, or the Centronics standard).

INFORMATION BANK   A large collection of data — also referred to as a data bank. The New York Times, for example, maintains such a "bank." One increasingly important use for home computers is connection, via telephone, to such electronic encyclopedias. If you intend to use your personal computer as a "remote terminal" for such a service, check to see that it will accept a *modem* (a device allowing a computer to use the phone) and will function correctly with the data bank which interests you.

INPUT/OUTPUT (I/O)   Communication between the computer and the outside world. Keyboards, display screens, disk drives, printers, even voice synthesizers, are all input/output devices.

INTERFACE   A connection. Probably the most technical aspect of computing is connecting devices together so that information can pass between them without errors. It is better to investigate what a computer can easily plug into (before buying it) than to try to make something work later on. Standard interfaces (built into the computer when bought) such as RS-232, IEEE-488, or S-100 allow you to add things (modems, printers, disk drives, etc.) fairly easily as you decide you want them. Some personal computers permit a great variety of potential add-ons (called *peripherals*). Voice recognition (your computer responds to your spoken commands) and synthesized speech (then it talks back to you in its own distinctive, machine accent) are making an appearance in the consumer market. You will probably want such accessories as they come along – and your computer's interface potential will be an important consideration.

INTERFACE MODULE   A device used by computers (with non-standard interfaces) to attach standard peripherals through standard interfaces such as RS-232.

KILOBYTE   1024 bytes (memory cells). A standard measurement of computer memory size, as in 16K (16,384 bytes). Sometimes abbreviated "Kb" or "K."

KEYBOARD   The most common way of communicating with a computer. It usually resembles a standard typewriter keyboard more or less.

LCD   An acronym for Liquid Crystal Display, a flat display where a black on white pattern can be electronically controlled to form symbols or shapes.

LIGHT PEN   A device which detects the X, Y position at which it is pointing on a TV screen. Used for program selection, or even on-screen "painting."

MEGABYTE   One million (1,000,000) bytes. Sometimes abbreviated as "Mb" or "M".

MICROPROCESSOR   A CPU which often contains additional memory cells. Increasingly included in appliances, vehicles, and machinery of all types. A machine which contains a microprocessor is called an *intelligent device* and is, in fact, an early, simple, robot.

MODEM   A device with which one computer can communicate with other computers over the phone lines. *Acoustic modems* transmit and receive data audibly through the phone handset. *Direct-connect modems* attach directly to the phone line, eliminating errors caused by environmental noise. They also cost more than acoustic modems, and can't be used with older telephones.

MONITOR   High quality computer display with finer resolution than a television, although most monitors are black and white.

NON-VOLATILE MEMORY   As opposed to RAM memory (which "forgets"), a type of memory that retains information when the power is off. ROMs, PROMs and EPROMs, fall into this category.

OPERATING SYSTEM   A program usually built into the computer which controls the operation of the computer, including input/output (I/O), and memory management.

PARALLEL   An *interface* which transmits information a byte at a time, as opposed to a (*serial*) stream of bits. Commonly used for printers, disk drives, and laboratory equipment.

PROGRAM   A list of instructions for the computer to follow. Making such a list is called *programming* and the person who makes the list is called the *programmer*.

PERSONAL COMPUTER   A computer made available for home use. In terms of power, distinctions between "personal" and "business" computers are becoming less meaningful. Home computing can be as powerful and as complex as you can afford.

PIXEL   Picture Element – the dots on a TV screen which, lit or unlit, form the picture.

PORT   An extension of the computer's internal circuitry, an *interface* which other devices can plug into, such as a printer port or an RS-232 port.

PRINTER   A peripheral device which produces written text. Three types of printers are usually used with personal computers: daisy wheel (letter-quality), thermal (low cost, uses special paper), and dot matrix (fast, can approach letter-quality).

RAM   Random Access Memory. Computer memory which can be changed. These kinds of memory cells hold your program in the computer until you are ready to use another program. The second program simply "writes over" the first one. By contrast, *ROM* memory is also in the computer when you buy it, but cannot be changed. It is created at the factory with information which you don't want to have to tell the computer each time you turn it on. ROM remembers how to print words on the screen, how to figure square roots, and so forth.

RESET KEY   Used to interrupt and re-start the computer. A cold *reset* wipes out all memory; it's like turning the unit off and back on. A "warm" reset key is even more useful – it can interrupt the computer when your "break" or "stop" cannot. Watch for the location of reset keys, you don't want to press it by mistake.

RFI   Radio Frequency Interference. The FCC has set new standards for the level of interference allowed. RFI from your computer could interfere with the television display, an important thing to watch out for if you plan to use a TV as your display screen.

RS-232   A common (industry standard) *serial* interface used to attach devices such as MODEMs, printers, and some disk drives to your computer.

SCREEN EDITING   The ability to change text (programs or data) directly on the screen, using *cursor controls.*

SCREEN EDITING KEYS   Special keys used for *screen editing*, such as keys with arrows used for *cursor control*, or keys with words such as *backspace* or *clear.*

SCREEN DISPLAY   This refers to the number of lines and columns of text which can be on-screen at a given time. It is expressed as lines x columns. For example, convenient preparation of written documents (called *word processing*) can benefit from a 24 x 80 display to permit an entire 8 1/2 x 11 sheet of paper to be represented on the screen at one time.

SCREEN RESOLUTION   Poor resolution will blur the images on the screen and make text hard to read. You can determine the quality of resolution by simply seeing if words appear crisp and clear on the screen or are shadowed and smeared. Resolution is measured in pixels

Glossary

(picture elements). 30,000 pixels is adequate for most graphics, 60,000 is better than average, and above 100,000 is called *high resolution* and is useful for such applications as fabric design and certain videogames.

SERIAL   An *interface* which transmits information bit-by-bit, rather than in whole *bytes* as a *parallel* interface does. The disadvantage is in speed: serial interfaces transmit *data* more slowly than parallel interfaces, as much as ten times slower. The advantages of serial interfaces are lower cost, simplicity of design, and decreased Radio Frequency Interference.

TELECOMMUNICATIONS   Sending information via wire or radio waves. More specifically, this term usually means computer-to-computer communication over distances, usually through telephone *modem* devices.

TEXT WINDOW   A small area, usually four lines of text, which appears at the bottom of a screen. This allows mixing text and graphics easily on the same screen.

VOICE   A single musical tone. A computer with multiple voices can play more than one tone simultaneously, as in a chord.

WHITE NOISE   A special sound effect similar to the "rushing" sound of a blank TV channel. It is often used to imitate the sound of gunfire or explosions.

WINCHESTER DISK   A *hard disk* designed for small computers.

Notes

If you've enjoyed the articles in this book, you'll find the same style and quality in every monthly issue of **COMPUTE!** Magazine. Use this form to order your subscription to **COMPUTE!.**

For Fastest Service,
Call Our **Toll-Free** US Order Line
800-334-0868
In NC call 919-275-9809

COMPUTE!
P.O. Box 5406
Greensboro, NC 27403

My Computer Is:
☐ PET ☐ Apple ☐ Atari ☐ VIC ☐ Other _____ ☐ Don't yet have one...

☐ $20.00 One Year US Subscription
☐ $36.00 Two Year US Subscription
☐ $54.00 Three Year US Subscription

Subscription rates outside the US:
☐ $25.00 Canada
☐ $38.00 Europe, Australia, New Zealand/Air Delivery
☐ $48.00 Middle East, North Africa, Central America/Air Mail
☐ $68.00 Elsewhere/Air Mail
☐ $25.00 International Surface Mail (lengthy, unreliable delivery)

Name _____

Address _____

City _____ State _____ Zip _____

Country _____

Payment must be in US Funds drawn on a US Bank; International Money Order, or charge card.
☐ Payment Enclosed   ☐ VISA
☐ MasterCard   ☐ American Express
Acc t. No. _____ Expires _____ /

234122

If you've enjoyed the articles in this book, you'll find the same style and quality in every monthly issue of **COMPUTE!'s Gazette** for Commodore.

For Fastest Service
Call Our **Toll-Free** US Order Line
800-334-0868
In NC call 919-275-9809

COMPUTE!'s Gazette
P.O. Box 5406
Greensboro, NC 27403

My computer is:
☐ VIC-20 ☐ Commodore 64 ☐ Other _____

☐ $20 One Year US Subscription
☐ $36 Two Year US Subscription
☐ $54 Three Year US Subscription

Subscription rates outside the US:

☐ $25 Canada
☐ $45 Air Mail Delivery
☐ $25 International Surface Mail

Name _____

Address _____

City _____ State _____ Zip _____

Country _____

Payment must be in US Funds drawn on a US Bank, International Money Order, or charge card.

☐ Payment Enclosed ☐ VISA
☐ MasterCard ☐ American Express
Acct. No. _____ Expires _____ /

234122

COMPUTE! Books

P.O. Box 5406   Greensboro, NC 27403

Ask your retailer for these **COMPUTE! Books**. If he or she has sold out, order directly from **COMPUTE!**.

For Fastest Service
Call Our **TOLL FREE US Order Line**
800-334-0868
In NC call 919-275-9809

Quantity	Title	Price	Total
_____	The Beginner's Guide to Buying A Personal Computer	$ 3.95*	_____
_____	COMPUTE!'s First Book of Atari	$12.95†	_____
_____	Inside Atari DOS	$19.95†	_____
_____	COMPUTE!'s First Book of PET/CBM	$12.95†	_____
_____	Programming the PET/CBM	$24.95‡	_____
_____	Every Kid's First Book of Robots and Computers	$ 4.95*	_____
_____	COMPUTE!'s Second Book of Atari	$12.95†	_____
_____	COMPUTE!'s First Book of VIC	$12.95†	_____
_____	COMPUTE!'s First Book of Atari Graphics	$12.95†	_____
_____	Mapping the Atari	$14.95†	_____
_____	Home Energy Applications On Your Personal Computer	$14.95†	_____
_____	Machine Language for Beginners	$12.95†	_____

* Add $1 shipping and handling. Outside US add $4 air mail; $2 surface mail.

† Add $2 shipping and handling. Outside US add $4 air mail; $2 surface mail.

‡ Add $3 shipping and handling. Outside US add $9 air mail; $3 surface mail.

Please add shipping and handling for each book ordered.   _____

Total enclosed or to be charged.   _____

All orders must be prepaid (money order, check, or charge). All payments must be in US funds. NC residents add 4% sales tax.

☐ Payment enclosed   Please charge my: ☐ VISA   ☐ MasterCard
☐ American Express   Acc t. No. _____   Expires ____ / ____

Name _____

Address _____

City _____ State _____ Zip _____

Country _____

Allow 4-5 weeks for delivery.